E N T     I E S

# ADMINISTRATION

## Series Mission

To share new ideas and examples of excellence through case studies and other reports from all types of organizations, and to show how both leading-edge and proven improvement methods can be applied to a range of operations and industries.

ENTERPRISE EXCELLENCE |SERIES

# LEAN
# ADMINISTRATION

## Case Studies in Leadership and Improvement

Association for Manufacturing Excellence
(AME)

Most Productivity Press books are available at quantity discounts when purchased in bulk. For more information contact our Customer Service Department (888-319-5852). Address all other inquiries to:

Productivity Press
444 Park Avenue South, 7th Floor
New York, NY 10016
United States of America
Telephone 212-686-5900
Fax: 212-686-5411
E-mail: info@productivitypress.com

ProductivityPress.com

Material originally appeared in *Target*.

Library of Congress Cataloging-in-Publication Data

Lean administration : case studies in leadership and improvement : a compilation of articles from Target the periodical of the Association for Manufacturing Excellence.
    p. cm. — (Enterprise excellence series)
  Includes index.
  ISBN 978-1-56327-366-7 (alk. paper)
1.  Management—Case studies. 2.  Administration—Case studies.
3.  Leadership—Case studies. I. Association for Manufacturing
Excellence (U.S.) II. Target (Wheeling, Ill.)
  HD31.L3265 2007
  658.4'092--dc22

                        2007013328

11   10   09   08   07   5   4   3   2   1

# Table of Contents

Foreword . . . . . . . . . . . . . . . . . . . . . . . . . . . . . . . . . vii

Introduction. . . . . . . . . . . . . . . . . . . . . . . . . . . . . . . . xi


Section I: Leadership, Organization, and Training. . . . . . . . . . 1

**Chapter One**
HUI Expands Self-Directed Teaming to the Office. . . . . . . . . . . . 3

**Chapter Two**
Steelcase: Learning How to Implement Customer-Focused,
                Enterprise-Wide Lean . . . . . . . . . . . . . . . . . . . . 11


Section II: Improving Processes . . . . . . . . . . . . . . . . . . . 27

**Chapter Three**
Lean Goes Beyond the Production Floor  . . . . . . . . . . . . . . . . . 29

**Chapter Four**
Lean Office Events — Priceless Knowledge, Team Solutions . . . . . . 41

**Chapter Five**
Lean Success in an Administrative Environment . . . . . . . . . . . . . 51

**Chapter Six**
Lean Office: Mapping Your Way to Change. . . . . . . . . . . . . . . 63

**Chapter Seven**
Elgin Sweeper Co. Employees Clear a Path Toward Lean
Operations with Their Lean Enterprise System . . . . . . . . . . . . . 75


Section III: Lean in Healthcare. . . . . . . . . . . . . . . . . . . . 87

**Chapter Eight**
Metamorphosis: Healthcare's Ongoing Transformation. . . . . . . . . . 89

## Chapter Nine
"The Calling:" St. Vincent Hospice. . . . . . . . . . . . . . . . . . . . . . 109

Index . . . . . . . . . . . . . . . . . . . . . . . . . . . . . . . . . . . 129

# Foreword

## Lean Without a Product/Artifact

Most people realize that what we now call lean thinking is really a take-off on lessons from the Toyota Production System. Most people not actually making something in manufacturing have difficulty relating to a shop floor. They may never have seen one. Naturally, their question is, "What can concepts coming from manufacturing possibly have to do with me?"

Only a small percentage of people actually make something. Depending on which government figures you choose, only 12 percent of the U.S. workforce now works for a manufacturing company. Far from all of them are actually hands-on workers. To take dramatic examples, both Hewlett-Packard and Apple are classified as manufacturers, but neither has much domestic manufacturing. Only a tiny fraction of their U.S. employees are direct labor personnel. What do the rest of them do?

Most people work in service and administration. Some, as in utilities or construction, work in operational environments, but even there, much work is administrative. The potential to make a big difference improving non-manufacturing processes is huge.

But, given all this, most manufacturing companies begin their lean journey on the shop floor. That's where issues of waste and productivity receive the most scrutiny. The physical flow of work is usually easier to see. It is easy to assume that a physical artifact embodies value added; hopefully that's what the customer pays for. Therefore anything that impedes the production flow of artifacts is waste — something to eliminate. Besides, it slows the cash cycle, the time from when an order is entered until payment is received from a customer. Therefore, manufacturing and similar operations are prime areas for applying lean thinking in practice.

Service processes and service industries are a huge opportunity, for improving quality, delivery, productivity, and cost — and for directly improving the experience of customers.

By one definition, a service process includes a customer; map it end-to-end, and customer contact shows up in at least one box. And by an archaic definition, production processes are remote from customers, presumably to better concentrate on efficiency. Perhaps a customer on-site, seeing how things are really done, might have a lawsuit-beckoning accident– or at least be so appalled that she would cancel the order.

But that's not how quality-conscious companies are supposed to think. Most strive for customer satisfaction, or maybe even, like Toyota, for the ideal of zero unsatisfied customers. That's seldom achieved merely through possession of the artifact sold, but through customers' total experience that goes with it, including its functions, ease of use, repair process if needed — in sum, whether they consider life to be much better because they bought it. Therefore, all operating companies that have customers also have service processes, whether they are officially classified as a service company or not.

Service operations range from health clinics to tax advisories to criminal court systems, classified in various ways, profit or non-profit, etc. Some are associations like the Association for Manufacturing Excellence (AME). Classification by ownership is almost irrelevant to the rooting out of waste.

Over the years, *Target* has published a number of cases of applying lean thinking or other excellence thinking to non-manufacturing processes. We've also reported a few snippets about this in articles focused on manufacturing companies. For example, we reported that Guidant (now Boston Scientific) eliminated a huge fraction of their paperwork associated with pharmaceutical device manufacturing compliance by going back to the intent of the regulations, studying them, and figuring out simple ways to comply.

This snippet illustrates an important point about "administrative lean." Sorting out what does or does not add value is harder to simplify by making the assumption that all value is embedded in a physical product to be sold. Determining the customer for a process, and what adds value for them can be perplexing. An example from these readings is "The Calling," about St. Vincent's Hospice. Who are the customers, and what does satisfaction mean to them? For any administrative or service process, critically ask this question to identify waste that interferes with delivering that satisfaction.

To start your thinking about this, the classification below is

incomplete, and in no particular order, but it's a start:
- Necessary for customer education, information, development, or training
- Necessary for understanding what the customer needs or wants
- Necessary for convenience of the customer or to preclude trouble for them
- Necessary for legal or regulatory compliance
- Necessary for health and safety of any process stakeholder — customers, workers, service personnel, etc
- Necessary for local or global environmental sustainability
- Necessary to execute transactions with customers or suppliers
- Necessary feedback to check or improve the process.

The operative word in the list above is "necessary." A payment system can be highly effective, yet simple and fast. Or it can be a very ineffective, error-ridden, time-consuming, and a waste for any and all stakeholders. If no stakeholder is happy, it's a good clue that waste is abundant.

But the processes to scrutinize closely are control systems whose only "customer" is management. There may be good reasons, for example, to have audit trails. Later, they may be worth the trouble. If so, what is the simplest way to leave one? But beware of complex control systems. They may only be a symptom of much more waste that, were it eliminated, would not need any elaborate controls.

This kind of kaizen is apt to lead to revelations about systems sometimes held sacred, like cost systems. What effort goes into them; what results come from them; and what do they do that could not be done otherwise? A very productive exercise can be a series of kaizens about an annual budget process, questioning its purpose. But seeking to butcher a sacred cow is probably not the place to start. For most organizations, an order entry system is a less controversial beginning project; almost everyone would like to improve it. As a consequence a great many people can be involved in improving it, including some customers, so you can involve many people in learning how to take the waste out of an administrative process. At first, the key objective is to develop people working with "office processes" so that they become accustomed to routinely questioning old ways and looking for better ones.

This can dramatically change a company if you persist. For example, if a process is always subject to change, it makes a big difference in how the software supporting processes are designed. To understand what is happening and why, involve lots of people, including IT personnel, in early projects.

What you will find in the articles is how a number of different companies have applied lean thinking to various kinds of non-production processes. If you have never systematically attempted to improve "office processes," they may give you some ideas to start. Then don't become afraid of your own revolution. You'll make some mistakes; everyone does; that's part of learning. Work through them, keep going, and create some advances worthy of a *Target* article about them.

Robert W. "Doc" Hall
*Editor-in-Chief,* Target
*Association for Manufacturing Excellence (AME)*

# Introduction

Interest in applying lean principles to administrative operations as well as to manufacturing has been growing rapidly. As the concept of an entire lean enterprise gains ground, so has the desire for information about what has already been accomplished. This book provides a wide range of case studies to satisfy that hunger for information.

The chapters that follow originally appeared as articles in *Target* magazine, published by the Association for Manufacturing Excellence. Loyal readers of *Target* have long been familiar with its reputation for quality, in-depth case studies. The articles included here not only demonstrate the reasons for that reputation but also provide a range of insights into what it takes to achieve excellence in administrative processes.

It is almost a truism that lean cannot succeed without strong top management commitment. Therefore, the two chapters in the first section of this book are, appropriately, devoted to Leadership, Organization, and Training.

Chapter One details how the HUI company built on its experience applying lean to the shop floor to implement lean administration. This involved demonstrating commitment to a core set of values, adopting a different style of management, and creating teams in administrative areas.

Establishing senior-level teams and picking the right people for them were part of the approach to lean administration at Steelcase, an experience described in Chapter Two. In addition, project sponsors and value stream managers were selected, with value stream mapping workshops a central part of the strategy. Steelcase team members also learned the value of piloting changes before adopting them on a widespread basis.

The second section of this book, Improving Processes, encompasses five tales of companies in the forefront of lean administration.

Two companies — Rockwell Automation and The Antioch Company — are featured in Chapter Three. Both businesses tackled the challenges of bringing lean into non-production areas, learning a wide range of valuable lessons along the way.

The Antioch Company is also the focus of Chapter Four. But in this article, two Antioch managers describe their experiences first-hand, discussing in detail the types of waste that are repeatedly found in office situations. They also explain key process mapping steps, and the rules that must be followed to achieve success.

A British office of Waukesha Bearings embarked on a journey to lean administration, an adventure detailed in Chapter Five. That journey included overcoming cultural resistance, gaining a better understanding of what really constituted a value stream, experiencing "trystorming" rather than brainstorming, and overcoming an initial failure to achieve true imprfovement.

We return to The Antioch Company for additional lessons laid out in Chapter Six. Those lessons include how to identify when change is needed, how to analyze and update metrics, how to get started and how to sustain change.

And Chapter Seven details how the Elgin Sweeper Company built a lean culture throughout the business on the foundation of a 5S program carefully and methodically implemented in all departments.

The third and final section of this book reflects the spread of improvement activities in the healthcare sector. Two chapters comprise Lean in Healthcare.

Chapter Eight describes the experiences of several different healthcare organizations — ThedaCare and a collection of Iowa organizations involved in a variety of aspects of the healthcare system — in pursuing ways to save money, streamline operations and increase the quality of care.

And finally, Chapter Nine is a detailed case study of St. Vincent's Hospice in Indianapolis, where dedicated staff achieve improvements and a level of care that set a standard for this type of institution.

These three sections provide valuable insights into both how lean can be applied to administrative areas and what it takes for those efforts to succeed.

Each chapter is accompanied by a series of questions designed to help you think about what you need to do in your organization. The benefits of lean administration can be significant. This book can be one of your first steps toward achieving those benefits.

# Section I

# Leadership, Organization, and Training

# 1

# HUI Expands Self-Directed Teaming to the Office

## Growing the business by developing leadership in all areas

*Jim Tennessen and Lea A.P. Tonkin*

**In Brief**

Building on their success with shop floor teaming, HUI of Kiel, WI made the transition to office lean teamwork starting in 2002. Thanks to this approach — treating people as adults and providing them with the tools, freedom, and accountability to reach organizational goals — they've achieved increased throughput and other gains, as sales have continued to rise. Among their lessons learned: Commit to a long-term improvement process; leaders must change themselves so they don't get in the way of progress; align organizational strategy, marketing, organizational structure, decision making, and metrics; and make it safe for others to learn and try.

Give talented people clear-cut goals, the training and tools they need to reach those objectives and the freedom to make improvements happen in a teamwork environment, and you've got a winning combination. That's what senior leadership at HUI in Kiel, WI figured several years ago. The privately-held company, with about $20 million in annual sales, had been holding its own in its custom sheet metal markets back in 1999, yet cycle times and overhead costs were among nagging issues. Convinced that there had to be a better alternative to traditional management, CEO Kurt Bell, COO Dan Ruedinger, and other senior management looked for the means to create an environment that encourages risk-taking to grow themselves, their teams, and the business. Strongly positive results (increased throughput and other gains) achieved by production people then led to lean extension in

> ### About HUI
>
> Employees at contract manufacturer HUI, based in Kiel, WI provide services ranging from design and metal fabrication to powder coating, assembly, and supply-chain management. Approximately 110-115 people work at the non-union facility. Sales are approximately $20 million a year. Product lines include panels, enclosures, medical carts, various assemblies, and other products. The company's existed about 70 years.

office areas. HUI employees recently shared their story about the transition to office teaming during an AME workshop.

"In 1999, we had started with lean on the floor," Ruedinger said. "We shifted to work cells and also began making changes in strategy and in our customer base. At the same time we were working with a very traditional customer group that had a heavy industrial base. It was apparent to us that it was very difficult to differentiate ourselves to these customers and in these markets. As a response, we looked to integrate the advantages driven by lean into our sales and marketing strategies. This led us to a customer base filled with people looking for solutions to problems rather than parts that needed to be made. This change and the response that was required were the primary drivers to accelerating the teams and lean efforts in the office. We simply needed to be able to deliver more solutions in shorter time frames than ever before."

## Values Matter

Asking people to take a "leap of faith" toward team-based, lean operations had brought faster cycle times and cost savings in production. This shop floor lean experience helped to pave the way for lean office operations starting in 2002. Yet management realized that their commitment to core values in day-by-day activities as well as their vision of success would continue to play a major role in acceptance of new ways. HUI's core values and vision are shown in Figure 1.

## The HUI Improvement Model

HUI's continuous improvement model is based on a three-way combination of their strategic position, lean concepts, and what they describe

## HUI's Core Values and Vision

### Values

- Integrity. Be honest with yourself, talk straight.
- Courage. Dare to think and act differently.
- Respect. "See the good" in others; trust and act accordingly.
- Passion. In what we do and who we are.
- Growth. Learn from our mistakes.

### Vision

- HUI will be the company of choice in all that we do today and tomorrow.
- Sell our story, not product. Tell us what your problem is and how we can help you.

**Figure 1.**

as "Murray/Adulthood" concepts. The company's strategic position, described by Ruedinger, is to "seamlessly integrate speed and expertise in design, manufacturing, assembly, and supply chain solutions to help customers achieve their goals."

The Murray/Adulthood concepts (developed by Pat Murray) contrast sharply with the traditional "military model: of top-down, centralized authority — "do as you're told." Instead, people are treated as adults and encouraged to use their knowledge, skills, and creativity to achieve organizational goals. HUI employees were coached in these concepts by former team member and current outside consultant Eric Coryell. "He introduced the idea that people, like pack animals, are constricted by their fear of being separated from the pack," said Ruedinger. "When they are afraid, they don't speak up. So our general premise is that we coach people on how to talk about tough stuff — problem-solving issues, differences of opinion, teamwork, etc. We also do onsite and offsite team-building and training on individual learning styles, communication, and problem solving." In turn, HUI people use these skills and understanding to build overall performance-boosting capabilities: ownership of results, creativity, agility, and decision-making speed.

"Adulthood" challenges all employees — including senior management — to better their performance, said Ruedinger. Key adulthood qualities are shown in Figure 2.

**Adulthood**
- Create an environment where people can be adults
- Growth — try, learn from mistakes, trust
- Transfer ownership of results
- Build teams
- Create a learning- and growth-based company.

**Figure 2.**

## Leadership/Coaching

Leaders need to evaluate what they want out of lean reorganization, advised Ruedinger. "It's more about the growth of people who work with you than simply focusing on your own growth; you can't fake that," he said. "Most people don't get to leadership in business without being doers and tellers. Yet instead of telling people what to do, leadership needs to coach and teach, and to get people to ask good questions. You also need a longer-term perspective. Daily, you are making an investment for the future.

"At certain times, it can be tempting to go back to the old way. But after this month, you may then need to tell people what to do again. If you had let them make their own decisions — including some mistakes — then hopefully they will make better decisions as time goes on," he added.

The executive compared this approach to a sports model. "The coach doesn't play in the game," he said. "Their job is to prepare players for particular situations. Then the player executes it when the opportunity arises. My job is to prepare people on our teams — not to throw the pass."

## Organizational Structure: Teaming, Eliminating Obstacles to Improvement

Team-powered activities in the office and shop areas keep the improvement wheels turning. Ruedinger said senior leadership learned several years ago, through experience in shop floor teaming, that "your organizational chart and management structure are the biggest obstacles to improvement. We would rather invest in teams than in managers," he said.

After they'd "gone cellular" on the shop floor, HUI production people working in teams had learned how to make most of their products within a day or two. Yet overall leadtimes dawdled at one or two weeks. That led to the conclusion that leadtimes were not necessarily a shop floor issue. So HUI turned to "office lean" in 2002. Teaming seemed the way to go. Good choice. Since then, the company's Customer Business Development (CBD) teams succeeded in trimming waste (and cost) from their work flows (invoices, engineering drawings, etc.)

Each of the two CBD teams comprises nine people from sales, customer service, engineering, purchasing, and accounting functions. "Each team has its own group of customers, rationalized once a year. We are a job shop so they are not organized by product line," Ruedinger said. Earlier attempts to organize teams along geographical lines didn't work well. The teams each have roughly ten customers and $10 million in sales.

Asking questions about ways to sequence their work in line with customer demand and their takt time helped the CBD teams (over time) to streamline processes. "We didn't rock anyone's world too bad. We started small, with customer service and engineering," said Ruedinger. "Customer service people had been running up and down the hall, asking engineering people questions. It made sense to combine them in the same location. Then people realized how much time was spent looking for purchasing people, so we added them to the team. Sales and accounting people were added to the teams so we could end the shuffle back and forth."

CBD teams run one-to-three shifts to coordinate with the shop floor. Part-timers work according to demand. The teams develop their own (U-shaped) layouts and visual boards.

One of the tools used by CBD teams in their lean efforts is identifying their "products." These products range from estimates and quotes to engineering documents/drawings, shop packets/routings, and invoices.

The teams now have common goals and collaboratively solve their mutual problems. "They were already doing various smaller pieces of the process. Now our teams are self-accountable and self-sufficient in the office and on the floor," Ruedinger continued. "People are treated as adults. We don't tell them what to do, but what we want to accomplish. Teams create their own revenue goals for the year and understand how they can make it happen. They leverage their skills, knowledge, and talents to do that. Management and layers of organization would slow things down. We would rather invest in people on these teams than in managers. All of our teams are self-directed."

## More Transitions

Not everyone accepted the new ways. Some managers took on other jobs or left, and engineering people who didn't like the new structure also left over three years' time. Reasons why culture change is difficult include loss of control, confusion about the need for change, the need for upper-management buy-in, and some people just don't "get it." Ruedinger suggested that senior leadership find ways to reward people who learn and use improvement concepts, and also accept that the five percent of the workforce resistant to change may have to leave. Shop employees at HUI are paid based on skill level. All employees get a percentage of profits (shared equally).

HUI now hires using different criteria than in the past. A senior manager, human resources, and a team member (if appropriate) screen candidates. They narrow the field to three individuals. Criteria include team skills, self confidence, a willingness to express an opinion, conflict resolution skills, growth-minded (not just willing to stay in a comfort zone), in addition to technical skills and experience. Then the team that the job candidates may join interviews the three job finalists and hires the one they think is the best fit. The teams can also fire people if needed and do evaluations of each other's job performance.

Lean training (internal) for office as well as floor employees is part of the mix. They've also been trained in communications and facilitation, learning to take a risk when they believe it's a good call. Office folks spent time identifying ways they could apply the same lean principles for cycle time reduction, etc. as used on the shop floor. Every team member has a training plan for the year (they vary from year to year depending on current or projected challenges). Senior managers evaluate teams' (office and the floor) performance each month and then work most intensely with the three teams struggling most.

Office CBD teams aim to standardize layouts and devise new continuous improvement projects, as do their counterparts in the shop. "Right now, we are trying to decide if we need both purchasing and customer service people on each team or whether to have two customer service/purchasing (a combined job) people on a team," said Ruedinger.

## Office Team Results

The teamwork at HUI is a work in process, according to Ruedinger. Yet early CBD efforts to eliminate wasted steps, emails, calls, and paperwork have brought substantial reductions in overhead. "In 2004 versus the previous year, we had more than a 15 percent increase in throughput sales per day per person on each of our teams," the executive said. "Sales are up 16 percent per person versus the previous year, so we are able to generate more business with the same amount of people.

"The average person in a traditional office spends an astronomical amount of time emailing and calling and waiting for a response. The best example is to look at how long receivables traditionally sit waiting to be collected for customer service and accounting and engineering to get together and settle issues. It can take weeks," stated Ruedinger. "In our setup, these people sit within 15 feet of each other and they resolve issues faster. Days' sales outstanding and leadtimes have come down significantly.

## True Change

"We don't stress measurements, although leadtimes are down and throughput is up in the office; culture change has to come first. You can walk into a situation and improve it on a short-term basis, but you may not have effected lasting change. For example, I could do a kaizen event and reduce cycle time, but I may have shifted work to purchasing or another area," he continued. "The only way to gain true change is to change the structure and dynamics of a group. I focus on issues such as how are we doing with revenue, throughput, and cash generation — not micro stuff."

Asked what's on the horizon for continuing improvements, Ruedinger said, "We're making this up as we go along. We try to emphasize that if you put everyone in the same room who can set their own goals for order to cash and cycle time, progress will happen. Our overall goal is to grow the business about ten percent a year and we've been successful in that. We realize that there is a need for ongoing change, and that without pressure from our customers, change doesn't happen."

## Lessons Learned

Dan Ruedinger and Kurt Bell offered a number of "lessons learned" from the HUI lean experience to date:

- Critical leadership skills include committing to a long-term improvement process, providing vision, following through during the hard times, providing resources, and not swerving from your goals (no "flavor of the month" fads).
- Before trying to change others, leaders need to change themselves — they may be the biggest stumbling block to progress!
- You get what you structure for and what you tolerate; evaluate your own organizational needs, and then commit to progress as a never-ending "journey."
- Align your organization's strategy, marketing, organizational structure, decision making, and metrics.
- Make it safe for others to learn and try.
- There is no single prescription for success. Challenge your paradigms and find what works best in your organization.

*Jim Tennessen of Tennessen Associates, Inc. is based in Minneapolis, MN and is the AME North Central Region president. Lea A. P. Tonkin, Woodstock, IL, is the editor of* Target *Magazine.*

---

## Questions

Does your organization have cross-functional teams? Do they receive the proper training and encouragement? Are they focused on particular products?

Have you encountered resistance to change? Do your managers understand the need to step back and let the team make decisions?

Do your hiring criteria include team skills, conflict-resolution skills, etc.?

Are your goals and strategies aligned throughout your organization?

# 2

# Steelcase: Learning How to Implement Customer-Focused, Enterprise-Wide Lean

## Building momentum and involvement as lean extends to office areas.

*Lea A.P. Tonkin*

**In Brief**

As Steelcase employees extend customer-focused lean concepts beyond production into office and administrative areas, their initial efforts yield gains in cycle time reduction, cost, and productivity. Yet they recognize the need for long-term commitment to this reorganization, including support from senior management. Energy and interest are building as the lean efforts continue.

What happens when "lean" meets the administrative side of an organization that's already achieved dramatic improvements in production operations? Can processes for order entry, distribution tracking, and other elements be mapped, brainstormed, and then streamlined or otherwise improved as effectively as on the plant floor? As Steelcase, Grand Rapids, MI employees recently shared during an AME workshop, the answer is a resounding, "Yes!" Participants in the "Steelcase University" program learned how lean concepts are being used to develop flow cells, standardized work, kaizen (improvement) activities scaled to office processes, sequenced pull signals, visual management, and other reflections of this philosophy. Customer-focused improvements encompass cost, speed, and productivity gains, depending on the process.

## Senior Leadership Support

Right from the start, enterprise-wide lean demands support throughout the company, starting with senior leadership. "We are crossing all sorts

11

of functional and structural boundaries in this effort," said Nancy Hickey, senior vice president, chief administrative officer, and executive sponsor of the company's office lean initiative. "You have to have leaders at the top aligned in a cohesive point of view. That has been really helpful in our transition." For example, Hickey and three of the other top executives reporting to the CEO are the senior executive steering team (the lean action committee, or LAC). Their involvement in everything from selection of office lean consultants to monthly meetings with lean project teams and gemba (being where the action is) walks with the lean consultants reflect a consistent focus. "We need to show that we are clearly serious about enterprise-wide lean, by not canceling our meetings and by staying on our schedules, and keeping other commitments," Hickey said. "It's not just another 'program du jour.'"

Picking high-potential people as office lean consulting team (OLCT—originally four members, now six) members in January 2005 set the tone for the office lean activities. "We looked for people with experience in managing others, and pulled them out of our organizations for a year—a testament to our level of commitment," continued Hickey. "We also are building the knowledge and vocabulary that will help us understand lean and how it is applied. It requires a broader mindset about what lean can do—about better processes and better customer results.

"Most challenging but most rewarding is to look at cross-functional changes that are happening as we continue our lean office initiatives," she said. "We've tended to be functionally organized in this company. Yet when we look for lean improvements in order-to-cash and product development, for example, these projects cross over several functional areas. You, and others in the organization, start to realize that what is happening in other companies affects your own activities and affects how we meet customer needs." Special challenges include traditionally weak or absent end-to-end process focus and process measures.

## Structure to Support and Sustain Successful Lean Initiatives

Steelcase senior management understands that their organizational structure and environment must support and help to sustain lean improvement activities. Without such a governance process or accountability structure, lack of clarity or political conflicts can lead to failure. Each administrative area targeted for a lean project has a designated project process sponsor (generally a vice president) with authority to direct project action. A value stream manager (or managers) for a segment (or segments) upstream or downstream of the selected project area helps to shepherd the project to completion. A vice president from the finance area whose responsibilities include coordination among projects in the order-to-cash sector of the business as well as OLCT members (internal lean consultants) support these individual activities.

Three-day value stream mapping workshops in targeted processes typically launch a series of collaborative improvements. (Lean project phases are shown in Figure 1.) Participants include associates from the selected area as well as others—customers or suppliers, either internal to the company or from the outside, depending on the process — typically considered upstream or downstream processes, said David Mann of the OLCT. Mann said that, in the case of the sales organization, distributors or dealerships (independent businesses) may participate in the sessions. They map (see "Value Stream Mapping and Visual Control: What's Really Going On Here?") current and future processes, evaluate potential remedies for problem or unnecessary activities, and develop a 90-day action plan to implement the desired future state.

Members of a decision panel (leaders such as the director, general manager, or vice president) whose areas are involved in or affected by a process) play a key role in oversight and approval of the project's progress. They join the project team on the second day of their workshop, asking questions about the nature of planned changes shown on the future state map. They discuss with the team whether the project should go further or pull back. After sometimes-pointed back and forth exchanges, panel members and the team come to agreement—and mutual commitment—on matters such as speed, scope, and specifics for the future state. This process builds the buy-in and understanding with the project team to set needed and attainable goals. "It is the idea of a process view overlaid on a functional organization," Mann said. "Lean projects are operating as virtual process operations in a real, day-to-day context of our functional organizational structure." The idea is to provide needed oversight and support for sustained success rather than single hits.

Progress checks help project teams keep improvement activities on track. Complex projects typically review their work with the decision panel at 30-day intervals. Together, they review actual progress versus plans, share what the team has learned in the past 30 days, and

## Lean Project Phases

**Preparation:** Office Lean Consulting Team (OLCT) and functional leaders agree on the scope of the lean project (end-to-end and functional; objectives; team members; logistics; etc.).

**Training:** The team participates in an Introduction to Office Lean class (half-day session).

**Current state:** The team develops and agrees on a well-understood map of the current situation (this phase and the next two phases continue over three days' time).

**Future state:** The team develops a proposed vision of a lean future state and reaches agreement with the decision panel to go forward.

**Planning:** The team develops a proposed implementation plan and reaches agreement with the decision panel on the plan.

**Implementation:** Step-by-step actions to achieve the future state.

**Kaizen:** Training the team on lean tools and applying them to the value stream (this phase and the next two phases continue for 90 days).

**Progress checks:** Reviewing efforts, weekly and monthly, to keep the project on track.

**Documentation:** Updating the value stream map to reflect new work and performance.

**Communication:** Sharing effort and new knowledge within the organization.

Figure 1.

discuss issues and potential solutions. Project managers, meanwhile, review progress (on order-to-cash, for example) each week with the coordinating order-to-cash vice president. Project teams use the Gantt chart section of single-page A3 project plan documents to track weekly progress. They also use the A3 to guard against "scope creep," identify obstacles and roadblocks, and record interim and final progress against project objectives and measurements.

"If a major improvement project takes a year, we segment it in 90-day increments," Mann said. "We look at the resources and support required, the objectives, and results. Teams, in the beginning, tend to plan for more lengthy improvement projects. Over time, the authorizing process approach flows down from the senior level, and responsibility for results ultimately flows upward. This dynamic helps define project segments in which cadence of progress can be more readily sensed, and in which the lean approach to learning through smaller quantities more frequently applies." He added that a key understanding as projects continue their work is that learning is cycled between the project team and decision panel, enabling needed adjustments (the old familiar PDCA, or Plan, Do, Check, Act). At the conclusion of the project phase of improvement, the project sponsor and the team report to the lean action committee about their objectives and achievements. Ongoing monitoring of process measures, and improvement activity, should continue.

Creating procedures to reduce handoffs and errors in a specific project, for example, is valuable to the organization. Over time, what becomes even more significant is opening eyes and understanding about the idea of further improvement opportunities, according to Mann. Project experience gives leaders, teams, and individuals the understanding and mindset that open the lean doorway a bit more.

## Value Stream Mapping and Visual Control: What's Really Going On Here?

Many folks in administrative areas may shy away from this step-by-step analysis of their activities. Traditional ways of doing things in the office are different from what's happening on the plant floor, they might say. Yet Steelcase personnel in various administrative areas, championed by senior leadership and coached/encouraged by internal lean experts (sensei), have found that Value Stream Mapping (VSM) serves as a useful tool in lean projects designed to more effectively meet customer requirements. Mapping helps to answer the three Toyota Production System (TPS) questions:

1) What is the process?
2) How can you tell if it is working?
3) What's the process to develop the answers?

"There is a huge value to mapping in administrative areas," said Jerry Schipper, director, Solutions Fulfillment Team. "First, it is an excellent learning experience for the people involved. It is surprising how often you will hear people say, 'Wow, I didn't know that is the reason we are doing it this way!' Even when people are seasoned in their jobs, it doesn't necessarily mean that they fully understand all the processes or use the best practices. Too often in office environments, people do their work in a way that seems most comfortable to them. But it may not be the most effective way or one that meets the needs of the organization and its customers."

Whereas manufacturing process maps generally are linear, office process maps often branch into multiple paths; many resources are shared; and metrics such as cycle times and yield are usually unknown. "Mapping is critical, and it can be ugly," Mann added. "The front end of many enterprise value stream maps looks like a spaghetti map of a production process in pre-lean state, with many crossed wires. There may be a lot of reverse flows, resulting from poorly specified requirements or a lack of standardization. You're uncovering sources of frustration. It's almost a cathartic experience—a very powerful thing."

Mann noted that VSM contributes to visual control of processes, a key element in lean activities. "Our work force is down 45 percent from four years ago. Many people are really stretched to cover processes that used to have twice the staffing. It is important to understand the activities of upstream and downstream neighbors. In turn, you determine where there are loop-backs, waiting, queues, rework, and other wasted activities ("Seeing the Process, and the Muda" in Figure 2). Mapping very clearly points to problems and helps to focus direction for lean enterprise improvements. We are working on this area, but we still are not very robust yet," he said. "We need to see the pace and the progression of work—not just in terms of what the work is, but comparing actual output (weekly, daily, or other increments) with expected output. If we were doing that, it would enable us to see process status more clearly. In turn, that would prompt us to take a much closer look at the work content and to see additional areas for improvement. We've made a lot of improvements, but we are working toward progress in that area."

## Reorganization for Better Customer Service: Solutions Fulfillment Team

Mapping marked the start of customer-focused reorganizations (the evolution continues) within Steelcase's Solutions Fulfillment Team (SFT). The main responsibilities for this group of approximately 140

## Seeing the Process, and the Muda

True "pull" may rarely exist in the office. The office lean project teams strive for:
- Eliminating non-value-added process steps and hand-offs
- Standards for releasing and sequencing work in the area
- Flow using standard processes.

The muda, or waste, revealed and eliminated through office lean initiatives may include:
- Over-production (starting a task without complete requirements, for example)
- Inventory (unnecessary emails and paperwork)
- Waiting
- Non-value-added processing (such as re-entering data between incompatible systems)
- Defects/rework/iterations of work
- Excess motion (walking to and from the copier or buildings, etc.)
- Transportation (sending mail between departments and other activities)
- Under-utilized people (no method to encourage or capture improvement ideas).

**Figure 2.**

employees are entry and management of dealer orders, from order receipt through delivery to the customer. Rick Hawley, SFT project manager, said the initial process maps created in 2004 by SFT personnel with corporate lean staffers revealed that there were opportunities, spread over many activities, to remove non-value-added (NVA) steps that slowed customer service.

"We looked at our current state map from order receipt to delivery, and suggested that we begin to group related areas or sub-processes of opportunity into improvement loops," Hawley said. "The first loop we evaluated was order acknowledgment. It involved the primary responsibilities of order entry and order management." This evaluation, started in 2004, was completed in August 2005. Now they're tackling the order scheduling loop. Additional loops identified for mapping and potential improvement ranged from the orders received loop to the customer-specified material (CSM—when a customer specifies a special fabric for furniture, for example), the special products loop (other than standard products such as over- or under-sized pieces or special configurations), the distribution planning loop, and the post-shipment loop.

One of the major changes resulting from the initial order acknowl-edgment loop mapping and analysis was reorganizing personnel into teams. "We had some team structure prior to VSM," Hawley said. "But what we pulled together was that order management reps and editors (order entry people), previously on separate teams, now are grouped in regional teams handling orders for particular areas of the country. Physically being located together eliminated inefficiencies — work being passed back and forth for clarification, for example. We eliminat-ed many emails, and also actual movement of people, and related wastes."

The changes did not stop there. "As we continued to look at how people were working together, we decided to combine the two (order entry and management) positions into one. Now, the same person who takes orders also handles changes," Hawley said. "That has helped our dealers resolve after-shipment and other issues that might occur." Approximately 140 Steelcase personnel were affected by the revamped work flow. About 400 dealers are served by the group.

## Start Small, Then More Broadly Roll Out the Changes

To backtrack a bit: The SFT reorganization did not happen overnight. First, a small pilot involving six reps and order entry people working in a controlled environment simulated "how the changes will work" and related issues. "Once they proved it could work, combining the two positions, we started implementing the change across the organi-zation, one group at a time, over a 90-day period," said Hawley. The pilot team, working with corporate lean resources, became advocates for the new ways. "They knew what worked, and they helped to sell the changes by training their peers," Hawley said.

Awareness training for reps, training in responsibility changes, etc. continued. Debugging aimed at eliminating waste, confusion, and other potential snags also proceeded, still in a closed environment.

"Our expectation was to maintain or improve our performance. A key measurement is how quickly we acknowledge a customer's order," Hawley continued. "We met this goal before we involved cus-tomers in the changes. Going into the continuous improvement (CI) effort, we had a three-day backlog of orders-to-acknowledgment.

Thanks to our reorganization, we reduced that time to one+ days." When there are special fabric orders, for example, there may be delays beyond a day.

"Among the lessons we have learned is to pilot changes before trying to implement them in day-to-day production," noted Hawley. "Prove out your thoughts. Think of CI; if it doesn't work well, it's easier to tweak the process in a pilot environment than with a large number of people. A phased effort worked well for our first and second pilots; as we implemented change, we moved from one region to another.

"We also learned with our first team that when you are consolidating steps in a process, you can build too many steps into one person. For example, at first we thought about adding logistics responsibilities to order entry and management, but that introduced a huge training challenge. The training recovery time was longer than we could support."

Another key learning was to keep communications as open as possible. "As we began and continued our lean effort, our leadership was communicating monthly and quarterly with everyone in the organization about what the pilot team was doing, including VSM efforts and other updates," Hawley recalled. "Now our lean group publishes a monthly newsletter, sharing updates on new teams being created and team activities (results and benefits)."

More previously identified CI loops are being targeted. "We also are looking at areas that support the big process and customer service that were not identified in our first VSM, for example a quality support team that deals with opportunities in post-shipment issues," Hawley said. "We may go back in six months and see how we can finetune our initial efforts. We are encouraged that improvements are starting to take hold."

# Product Data Management: Reducing Rework and Other "Interrupters"

Better customer service topped everyone's list of priorities in Steelcase's Product Data Management (PDM) area during recent reorganization efforts, and they can also report substantial success in related lean improvements. PDM employees develop marketing and manufacturing data, spec guides, and catalogs. Initial VSM activities documented "flow interrupters" or NVA steps (repeated transcription and re-entry of data, cross-checking errors, etc.) that bloated wait times between tasks. "We learned that some tasks stayed in our system for as long as nine months. We've learned how to reduce that time to about four-and-one-half months during the past two years," said Kim Harring, PDM team leader and senior product data analyst.

"In the past, we had stops and starts in the process. We'd lose focus when we took questions as far as we could, and then interruptions occurred," added Doug Benner, a PDM manager. "Now we have a new checklist for gathering all details we need on a project, so we don't start building until our information is complete."

Although the "people side" of cultural change in PDM accounts for significant streamlining results, Harring and Benner noted that tools such as electronic documentation boost performance improvements. "Before, hand-scribbled notes were used," said Benner. "We created tools like a product questionnaire to help determine whether a project is validated and completed, ready for the next step. We began to use binders, and then moved to online product information, reducing rework and other downstream interrupters that had caused problems when a product goes to the build lane before it was ready. Rework has decreased an estimated 25-50 percent. We are still infants in this process of improvement. We have years and years of opportunities for CI."

## Starting the Evolution: What Co-Location Is All About

Increasing momentum of cultural change will enable and encourage PDM folks to take advantage of earlier training about lean concepts. Employees in this area had also been introduced to reorganization, as Chuck Walker (now manager of the consolidated PDM organization) and others had spearheaded the integration of ten disparate departments such as the graphics team and the specs guide team.

Bringing departments together does not guarantee the elimination of time-consuming, wasted steps, however. Clumsy steps such as poor handoffs between shipping and marketing persisted, as people were working off different databases. "Walking through" a logical, step-by-step process was needed. VSM and kaizen (improvement) projects nudged the elimination of some unnecessary handoffs, and yet the realization persisted that lean efforts could be more successful.

"We began the evolution of our organization structure with co-location of personnel without redesigning our business process,"

Harring said. "We picked one group (the redesigned platform Pedestal Project—pedestals are the drawer units that support the work surface or desktop) as a pilot and learned more about how co-location works. People who had not worked together before learned how to work together and to make changes in a real-time setting. We expanded this effort, creating and living in a future state as it was being developed." Learning from plant engineers and others who had experience in collaborative database organization aided their progress. Manufacturing and marketing, among other areas, shared their database information, eliminating redundancies. Such collaboration enabled consolidation of more than a thousand iterations to approximately 40-50.

Building on the success of the first pilot (involving four people), they moved to a second pilot (ten people), and then expanded the co-location concepts to all projects. "At the same time we were learning how to be more effective in implementing these changes," said Benner. "We used PDCA—trying and studying different things to see what worked. We learned the value of a checklist versus tribal knowledge. We developed process documentation, visible progression of work, and standards for input quality. Our value stream organization was aligned to product categories. It was a high-focus, successful project. Through monthly management meetings and also 'town hall' PDM meetings and our sensei (lean teachers) from the corporate lean team, more managers became interested and began asking how we accomplished the changes.

"Cultural change is a big effort, however, and not everyone is initially receptive," he continued. "When the company tied visual control boards and lean metrics such as cycle time, flow interrupters, and rework to the performance plan, on an individual and team level, that was a key to greater acceptance."

Speed, cost, and productivity improvement momentum is building. For example, the old 29-week price adjustment process (extended to all products) shrank to four weeks as VSM projects and related post mortems uncovered wasted steps and delays. Also, in product graphics, a problem in earlier days was that graphics lagged getting into the marketplace by six months. Customer feedback indicated that new products did not launch well unless the graphics were available. "About nine months ago, we changed our process flow and added some staff. Now our graphics are released with the product introduction. Some customers would like to see pre-release product graphics, and we are working on that," Benner said.

Added Harring, "We have almost doubled our graphics outputs

during the past year. Cycle time decreased from 56 to 20 days in graphics, and productivity is up 470 percent. That's a huge benefit. We are moving to a pull system in graphics with a FIFO (first in, first out) production lane, based on hours per unit (HPUs)."

The corporate enterprise lean team has expanded to six working across the enterprise, up from the original two, based in large part on the success demonstrated in applying lean principles to the PDM process. The need for process definition and visual control continues to be critical. The basics such as documenting process steps, process mapping to reveal drifts from standard, controlled releases between work phases, and reduction in batch sizes demand attention. "We're not perfect by any means, but we follow up with performance evaluation and management attention every 90 days to six months, to make sure we are conforming to the standards we have developed and to look for new improvement opportunities," said Harring.

## Learning from Experience, Customers

Harring and Benner shared key "lessons learned" about creating and continuing focus on cultural change for better customer service. "When we got started, there wasn't any office lean training beforehand. Now, we recommend VSM and lean training before implementation," Harring said. "That eliminates misunderstandings when people are on different wavelengths of knowledge about lean.

"We've also learned to communicate more effectively about acceptance. Until people have lean experience, they ask questions such as, 'What are you doing with my job?' People were scared and protective of what they do, and they associated lean with cutbacks. Sharing information and training each other reduce the reluctance to change. It's important to understand, especially in the beginning, that it is OK to fail, instead of just saying 'This isn't going to work.' You need to get people to just try it and see where it takes us."

"The willingness to try new ways of working together eventually leads to an understanding that, if the changes fail, we learn from it," Benner said. "We still have a ways to go, however. About 50 percent of our people are still in lean training, so not everybody's there yet. Eventually, we can hand over the lean changes to our teams. They'll do kaizen projects in identified areas where we are still not getting the performance we need."

Targets include further reductions in cycle time and other

improvements that can trim the budget and improve customer service. Harring noted that a grassroots effort is aimed at more efficient information sharing with upstream processes. VSM activities are expanding to focus on the entire product launch process — trying to improve the customer experience.

"We have a customer satisfaction group that is evaluating how customers can more effectively use our deliverables," Harring said. "We want to learn what the dealers' issues are, and to get our own people into the field for a better understanding of the issues such as graphics. For example, we need more information about how our designers use information to plan our products, and then in turn more about how spec guides are developed and laid out. With our marketing group, we are learning how dealers in target markets such as New York are using our tools. As much as we are going electronic, we can't get rid of print materials, based on our meetings with dealer groups. About some of the things we offer, they have said, 'Put them in our hands more readily.' When we understand their needs, then we can fix things and make the dealers' lives a lot easier. This kind of research— staying close to our external customer — will be a continuing focus, to eliminate work-arounds and other issues for them."

Such efforts represent major cultural change. "A few years ago, people would have had a hard time understanding that lean concepts can be transferred from production to the office," Benner said. "Now we are continuing to learn about efficient process flow."

"We're not going to change the entire organization overnight," Harring said. "Toyota has been at it over 40 years. You need to have a lot of patience, because not everyone is going to adapt and get on the lean journey all at once. As other areas of company go through the lean process, it will add to our momentum."

## More Lessons Learned

The lesson of patience was seconded by enterprise lean team leader David Mann. "It is important for people in office areas to learn lean concepts, and to hear examples in office terminology," he said. "Examples from manufacturing are next to worthless in the office if the people you're talking with don't have experience in manufacturing. It's a different language in the office, and that's important to recognize—and respect — when working with office people." Mann said that, just as lean principles apply equally in the shop and the office, the lean sensei needs to regularly visit office areas where lean implementation is under way — a continuing process of developing deeper understanding of lean principles, and better eyes to see opportunity to improve.

Trying to rush the lean improvement process detracts from the focus on process, and ultimately, on producing improved results. It is something like putting an order into the system too early without concern for completeness and accuracy, in turn causing rework, delay in payment, or other problems. "Improvements in the office will be no faster than in the factory, and in some cases, you won't see results as quickly," Mann said. "Many office processes are not that discrete, and there are more shared resources — less dedicated to a single line."

Jerry Schipper added, "To be successful, you need clear ownership of the process, so that people know what they are responsible for. You also need clear, simple, appropriate metrics. There's the old saying, 'What you measure, you improve.' Establish the measurements, tweak them if they are not quite right, and religiously follow up on them. Also, training and communication are important. For an organization making a culture shift such as we are, you cannot scrimp on either one."

## Gaining Traction: "A Lot of Tough Work"

The Steelcase lean enterprise efforts encompassing office as well as factory applications will continue. Asked how mature the Steelcase office lean efforts are, after a couple of years' experience, Nancy Hickey responded, "It's more about pioneering at this point. We are creating processes and formats through a lot of tough work." She offered these suggestions for others pursuing enterprise-wide lean:

- If you are coaching someone, understand how long it will take to get the improvement momentum going
- You need milestones to move people's minds to a lean way of thinking, and sometimes measurements are more difficult at various levels
- Build experience and understanding with hands-on activities
- Give people the time and resources they need for specific projects, enabling them to get traction with improvements.

"We have set a stretch goal—looking for significant cost reductions, eliminating unnecessary work and more value-added work, (a smoother order-to-cash process, for example), better productivity, and other improvements," Hickey said. "We will keep moving against these goals.

"Other achievements are not as 'hard' as cash savings yet they are important," she added. "Since we have been working on adoption of lean in administrative and office areas, people are saying that they want to learn better ways to work. That is significant when you consider that from 2001 to 2003, we had a dramatic downsizing. Some people were shell-shocked, and many people were trying to do more with fewer people. Because of the lean enterprise approach, we now have more people asking for help doing their jobs—the energy and interest are building."

*Lea A.P. Tonkin, Woodstock, IL, is the editor of* Target *Magazine.*

---

## Questions

Are your top managers actively involved in steering your lean initiatives? Does each area designated for improvement have a project process sponsor? Do segments have value stream managers?

Do you have an internal lean consulting team?

Is value stream mapping an integral part of your projects?

On long-term projects, how often is work reviewed? Who conducts the review?

Have your lean initiatives led to any reorganization? Are you considering a lean reorganization?

How do you gather information about customer use of (and satisfaction with) your products or services?

# Section II

# Improving Processess

# 3

# Lean Goes Beyond the Production Floor

Rockwell Automation and The Antioch Company
share how-to, lessons learned.

*Dave Hagford, Ev Dale, and Lea A.P. Tonkin*

**In Brief**

Both Rockwell Automation and The Antioch
Company have had success in applying
lean methods to non-manufacturing areas.
Their lessons learned cover a wide range
of key issues, including management commitment, training, communication, and
expectations.

Been working on lean in
production areas and
wondering how to
break the news to office-
dwellers that they're next on
the lean implementation list?
Having qualms about lean implementation in administrative areas of
your organization? Minnesota associates at two companies—Rockwell
Automation and The Antioch Company—recently shared their experiences in the Minneapolis AME workshop, "Application of Lean
Enterprise Principles & Processes Beyond the Production Floor." The
event included a tour of Rockwell Automation's facility in Eden
Prairie, MN. This article provides selected details from the workshop
presentations and tour.

## Rockwell Automation: Aiming for Leadtime, Cost, and Inventory Reduction Targets

After learning from a sister operation within Rockwell Automation
about implementation of Integrated Cost Reduction (ICR) and its merit

## About The Antioch Company and Rockwell Automation

**The Antioch Company,** based in Ohio, includes several business divisions. Antioch Publishing, based in Yellow Springs, OH provides bookmarks, bookplates, journals, diaries, stickers, and other products sold through retail bookstores, gift stores, and mass market retailers, and also sells custom made-to-order products for retailers and distributors; Webway sells photo albums and pages through retail stores and direct to the customer; Creative Memories based in St. Cloud, MN is a direct selling arm—independent consultants teach how to preserve family stories in scrapbook photo albums and they also offer The Creative Memories Collection® line of scrapbook albums and supplies; Creative Memories International sells variations of U.S. products in Australia, Canada, Taiwan, the United Kingdom, Germany, Japan, and other markets; zeBlooms of Kansas City, KS is a direct selling enterprise that imports and distributes silk flowers and provides floral arrangement instruction through home shows. The company's manufacturing facilities are in Yellow Springs, OH; St. Cloud MN; Sparks, NV; and Richmond, VA.

**Rockwell Automation** is a leading global provider of industrial automation power, control, and information solutions. The company encompasses leading brands in industrial automation including Allen-Bradley® controls and services, Dodge® mechanical power transmission products, Reliance Electric™ motors and drives, and Rockwell Software® factory management technologies and applications that help companies efficiently manage interaction with customers. The Milwaukee, WI-based company employs approximately 22,000 people and serves customers in more than 80 countries.

in lean improvement activities, associates at the company's Eden Prairie facility attacked related leadtime, cost, and inventory reduction targets. ICR incorporates up-front target setting, design-to-cost, optimization of supply base, lean value chain, platforming (standardize and reuse parts, scale inexpensive solutions), etc.

"We began in June 2002 with this approach," said Dale Kersten, supply chain manager at Eden Prairie and also ICR project manager. "We were looking for a percentage reduction in cost, for example, on a motor line." Employees at the plant make servo motors for applications such as packaging equipment, etc.

ICR involves a detailed, comprehensive analysis about both product and process. Practitioners systematically evaluate and take action as needed on all factors directly or indirectly affecting the product margin. Kersten said it can be applied to new product development and continuous improvement (CI), with sustaining and transition project team members. Using ICR, look at the entire spectrum of a product life cycle, from raw material acquisition until the product reaches the final customer. "The tools may look familiar, but it's how they are used and bundled together where power is gained," said Kersten.

A cross-functional approach is essential to ICR success. The core team at Eden Prairie, for example, included manufacturing engineering, design engineering, and marketing representatives in addition to Kersten. "We had the benefit of core team members from another Rockwell facility in Mayfield Heights, OH who 'parachuted' in and gave us training," he said. "They were our mentors, and we updated with them on a weekly basis for the next few months, and still can call on them for support." The core team reported to the director of operations and group vice president.

"Our main goal as a team was analysis and recommendation," Kersten said. Although the team was responsible for defining a business roll-out plan, selecting and approving targets, monitoring programs, and making resources available for related projects, they understood that ICR success depended on buy-in from all associates. Kersten recalled, "We had five or six brainstorming sessions, and asked them, 'Let's put everything on the table; what would you do to improve this process?'" These discussions brought together employees from related areas. For example, manufacturing engineering and manufacturing supervisors were in one session, while another group of brainstormers included production control, schedulers, and purchasing.

"We got more than 200 improvement ideas during a week of meetings," according to Kersten. "As a team, we (the core team) sat down and discussed what was possible, what we had information about, and other factors affecting project selection."

## Improvement Target Selection

Among the criteria used in selecting targets for ICR projects: Look for a potentially significant financial payback (Is it important to your business?), determine whether there are enough "rocks to turn over," choose targets over which project participants have significant control, select timely topics (ramp-up, mid-life "kicker," etc.), and buy-in awareness.

Rockwell Automation's Idea Qualification Level (IQL) analysis helped team members sift through and prioritize potential project suggestions (see Figure 1). A Level 1 idea is accompanied by the description with a projection of cost savings potential. At Level 2, an idea's plausibility has been checked and more data are made available. Solid, confirmed ideas rank Level 3; required change is under way at Level 4; and the idea is fully implemented at Level 5.

When the operation's ICR governance team perceives Level 4-5 ideas are in the works, they hand these ideas to a value engineering (VE) team to verify the improvement ideas. Additions and other modifications happen at this stage. Not all ideas will be given the green light; ideas are selected based on what seems to offer the best potential improvements, work "on their plate," etc. This idea qualification process ensures that there's a steady stream of viable ideas "on the shelf" for implementation, said Kersten.

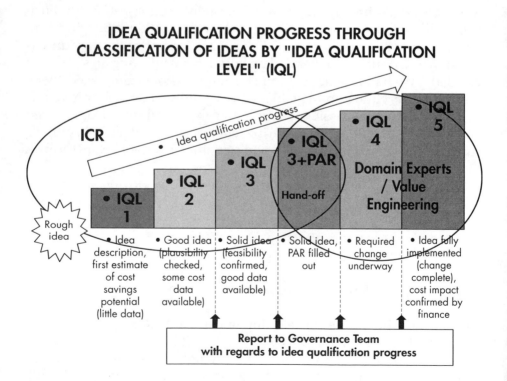

**IDEA QUALIFICATION PROGRESS THROUGH CLASSIFICATION OF IDEAS BY "IDEA QUALIFICATION LEVEL" (IQL)**

Figure 1.

## Mind Set That Change is Good

ICR project team members reviewed corporate resources as well as resources available at the plant level, and then created about a dozen implementation teams. For each project, they laid out a timeline and specified the skills required among team members. Teams progressed during the next several months to trim costs, reduce inventories, and decrease leadtimes.

Since the company has been training associates in lean concepts for several years, the groundwork had been laid for ICR change, said Kersten. "People already knew about value stream mapping, how to run successful team meetings, etc.," he said. "That really helps. People at this facility have the mindset that change is good. There is not a lot of resistance to change because change is part of our culture."

Results so far from ICR projects are encouraging, said Kersten. Cost reduction targets have been met. Eden Prairie inventories, both raw and finished goods, have decreased approximately 35 percent. Meanwhile, leadtimes for motor production decreased from 30+ days to just over seven days (domestic market) for the August 2002-March 2003 Period. Additional CI projects, perhaps selected with the assistance of people trained through the corporate "lean masters" program, are on the improvement agenda.

## Lessons Learned

As Kersten and fellow members of the ICR team continued to work with associates on needed changes, their experiences brought several "lessons learned:"
- Total commitment from upper management is a must.
- Assure that project staffing and other needed resources are in place. Key staffing functions (varying according to the program target) should be designated; rotate project team members with needed skills as appropriate; budgeting should be in place. Pull people out of their regular work for the project planning and more intense implementation phases.
- Communicate continuously about projects, overall objectives, and results. A weekly newsletter, employee meetings, etc. help to keep the momentum for change strong. Flow information up and down the organization for better buy-in and support.
- Don't limit your expectations. "We had residual improvements

that were not part of our original targets," Kersten said. "For example, we were curing a product for eight hours a day in an oven; associates suggested that we cure the product at night when energy prices are cheaper. If something can be implemented now, go ahead with the change as quickly as possible."

- Some project aspects may take longer than expected. For example, a competitive analysis step in a cost reduction project required unexpected time.

## The Antioch Company: "Requests Keep Coming In"

Things can get dicey when you're introducing lean concepts where traditional methods rule. Thanks to initial successes at The Antioch Company in St. Cloud, MN, lean momentum—requests for lean projects and related results—continues to grow. "We had been using kaizen blitzes to improve operations in the shop, and we felt that we had tools that could also be used in the office," said Jane Mobilia-Witte, senior materials manager. "We started in February 2002 in the office area with lean events, and now we've completed projects in accounts payable, the capital expenditure request process, new product development for the album-making process, the international portion of the business, etc. The requests keep coming in."

The lean office concept is viewed as a grass roots effort to manage growth without adding bureaucracy, according to Kristi Huls, engineering services manager. "We have a lean office department, but we do not use a lean steering committee. We have the flexibility to go where we are needed and to tailor our programs to meet the needs and schedules of the people working on the projects," she said.

Lean office event preparation includes initial goal development (cost reduction, faster cycle time, etc.); team formation (people involved in the process and asking outsiders and customers for an objective view of the process, too); and ordering needed supplies, meals, and gifts. The events are scheduled for two to four days (action items left at the end of the event are given target completion dates and assigned accountability when the event closes).

Participants (process experts, "novices" who are new to the process, support people who understand the process, decision makers, etc.) in the lean projects typically receive one hour's training at the start of each lean event. "The main objective is to understand what their roles are and what is expected of them during the event," said Huls.

When the lean event team gets started, they finalize goals and then interview people involved in the process they're focusing on. "It's an effective way to bring out new ideas," Huls said. All ideas generated are documented.

Team members interview process workers. They go to work areas or invite these associates to the meeting for discussions, writing down ideas as they talk.

## Process Mapping

Process mapping is a key element of the lean office events. A current state map is created using data from the interviews. The facilitators review the map with the team to check for accuracy and then discuss whether the activities they've documented add value (color coding on the process maps aids the evaluation). Value-added (VA) activities such as order-taking, creating a bill of material, etc. are critical to the process and are activities which the customer would be willing to wait or pay for.

In some cases, up to 98 percent of the activities have been classified as non-value-added (NVA). The team reviews the NVA activities to determine if they can be eliminated or minimized without reducing the value of the product or service to the customer. Undefined process flow, low-value meetings, fire-fighting and expediting, as well as errors, rework, and correction loops are among the types of NVA time-wasters revealed through process mapping. Other non-value-added (NVA) activities include to do queues (TDQ), walking to regularly-used materials and equipment, undefined roles, waiting for information, and unnecessary emails.

Huls and Mobilia-Witte said this mapping process of the current state puts everyone on a level playing field when process changes are being considered; generates understanding and awareness of the process; generates discussion of unresolved issues; and reveals the details that otherwise would creep into your future state process.

## Visualizing, Implementing Improvements

After the process mapping yields ideas for improvements, the project team visualizes alternatives to the current process. They ask customers about what is important to them, identify individual or process obstacles, and look at NVA activities on the current-state map (asking, "Why?" five times for NVA activities). The team proposes future state solutions, which are evaluated by the team.

The team creates a future state map, constantly asking if there is a better way to meet customer requirements (mindful of goals such as no piles, no waiting, reduced handling of paperwork and information, use of standard operating procedures, work triggers [preferably visual], continuous flow through the process, designated work sequences, and other goals). Once the future state is created, the action items are reviewed for validity to the new future state and are assigned to the team members. A follow-up meeting is scheduled within one or two months of the event.

## Accounts Payable: "A Willing Guinea Pig"

Accounts payable was "a willing guinea pig" for a lean office project at Antioch, said Mobilia-Witte. The team reviewed 14 different processes such as state and federal tax, royalty payments, expense reports, paying suppliers, etc. The processes were mapped. Improvement actions were selected and launched. "We took out 60 percent of the activities and streamlined quite a bit—less filing of records, etc.," Mobilia-Witte said.

"We challenged their beliefs about traditional activities such as keeping records," she continued. "For example, they made a photocopy of every check and deposit record. They attached the copies to the related invoice and packing slip. We challenged why the packing slip needed to be routed to accounts payable and stapled to the invoice, when only two percent of invoices needed extra attention to reconcile the amounts. The project team decided that the receiving department would hold the packing slips, and if they were needed, accounts payable would request a copy; this change eliminated a lot of copying, filing, and stapling."

Another change implemented as a result of the lean event is that all invoices and expense reports are now filed by check run rather than by supplier or individual name. A report is now printed stating all the check information and it is filed with the invoices and expense reports. "We estimate that this change saves copying and filing and stapling time at about eight hours a week," Mobilia-Witte said. "Also filing was the least-liked job in the department. Now they file by date and they switched from a batch process of sorting invoices to one-piece flow, speeding processing time. The new system also helps us meet discount dates on invoices."

"We also found a process (direct deposit for sales consultants) that didn't belong in their department," Huls said. "The team met with the consultant services department to discuss the process move. Consultant services agreed to take on the process and the associated file requirements."

## Streamlining the Capital Expense Request Process

Another example of process improvement through lean office team activities is Antioch's capital expense request process. It used to be bogged down by extensive policies for sign-offs in many different functions. Depending on the type of request and the dollar amount, such requests funneled through the plant manager in most cases, and then as needed through functional managers, maybe another vice president, perhaps the president and even the board of directors. Even a simple one could take a week or two and an "immense" amount of paperwork handed off manually throughout the chain of approvals. Engineers had to figure out what plant to go through and get documentation to the appropriate site.

"We estimated that it took an average two weeks to get a capital request approved," said Mobilia-Witte. "The team recommended making the approvals electronic, which we are in the development stage of implementation. We are projecting the approvals will be down to two days. The information technology (IT) people and other functional areas are working together to assure that all appropriate information is provided and that required information is available and usable." Training will be required to help everyone. Events such as this one may take two or three months to reach completion, but the efforts are rewarded by improved flow.

What's next for lean office processes at Antioch? Project requests keep rolling in. "Also, we're trying to learn how to dollarize the intangible benefits," said Mobilia-Witte.

## Sharing Experiences

Mobilia-Witte and Huls shared several suggestions for lean improvement projects, based on their experiences:

- Training is a must. This training helps team members understand why they are a part of the event and what they can contribute.
- Team members must have decision-making authority to make process changes in their area of influence.
- Team members should be focused on the process, not taking long breaks to return to their desks for phone calls and other projects. "You need to find a way to keep them engaged in the event."
- The interviewing process required for process mapping is a draining, but worthwhile activity.
- Focus on the process, not individuals. Also, focus on process improvement rather than simply eliminating process steps (some people find that concentrating on elimination of the traditional process stems is threatening or distracting).
- Facilitators must be unbiased and willing to change direction to meet the goals. The team, not the facilitators, must have ownership in the future state.
- Real change only happens when there is team participation.
- Follow-up meetings are essential.
- Event results are not always quantitative—many are qualitative. "We no longer have a goal of eliminating 50 percent of process activities," said Mobilia-Witte and Huls. "The lean office process usually results in 20–90+ percent reductions."
- Keep lean office processes (and solutions to problems) simple. For example, simply questioning emails (Are they needed? Are people on the distribution list the right people to receive the information? Is the information what people really want and can use?) can help to streamline processes.

*Dave Hagford is CEO and president of Creative Business Coaching, Edina, MN. Ev Dale, Dale & Associates, Minneapolis, MN, is a member of the AME North Central Regional Board. Lea A. P. Tonkin, Woodstock, IL, is the editor of* Target *magazine.*

---

## Questions

Do you have criteria for selecting targets for improvement?

Do improvement project plans have timelines and the skills required from team members?

Do you make sure the resources are available for an improvement project?

Do you communicate continuously about improvement projects?

After mapping, does your project team visualize alternatives and map a future state?

Do you have follow-up meetings?

# 4

# Lean Office Events—Priceless Knowledge, Team Solutions

Office waste uncovered at The Antioch Company.

*Jane Mobilia-Witte and Kristi Huls*

## In Brief

After experiencing success with lean initiatives on the production floor, employees at The Antioch Company created Lean Office Events for other areas. They developed rules for success, mapped process, and learned that many wastes are repeated over and over. Ultimately, they created a Lean Office Department.

Lean, Lean, Lean. We hear and read about it all the time, and we even practice the concepts in our plants, but what about the office? At The Antioch Company in St. Cloud, MN,[1] we asked the same question. We watched the amazing results from the lean initiatives in production and wondered how we could do the same in the office. The result—the Lean Office Event. After facilitating several of these events, we want to share our "lessons learned" about some of the typical wastes we see in office processes and the benefits from lean office events (see Figure 1).

The Lean Office Event was not a management-driven program, but rather a program developed by employees with the objective of taking the waste out of the office environment. The Antioch Company is an employee-owned company, so making changes that improve what we do goes to the bottom line, which is shared with the employee owners. So why wouldn't you want to make changes in your office process? It wasn't so simple.

The Antioch Company employees had their first office lean event in February 2002. This was a new concept to all employees, as well as the facilitators. As facilitators, we did extensive preparation, but we were still "winging it" because it was a new process. The team, which

# What a Lean Office Event Can Do For You

**Figure 1.** Benefits of lean office events.

consisted of ten individuals, also did not know what was expected of them. In a sense, they were the guinea pigs for the lean office concept. When you are in a new environment, many times defenses go up. In this case, many individuals became defensive as the group learned every detail of what they did and the team questioned them with "why." There were tears shed during the first event.

As facilitators, we learned so much from the first event. We have held 20 events since February 2002 and we are constantly tweaking the lean office concept to accommodate what we learn from each event. Instead of defensiveness and tears, the teams are now excited and anticipating the changes.

The lean office event concept is quite simple. First you develop the scope, set goals, complete a high-level map of the process in focus (see the "Process Mapping" box), interview the people involved in the process in detail, map the process, and then develop the future state. Any idea or issue that comes up during the event is documented and may become an action item once the future state map is complete.

**Process Mapping**

1. Interview—gather the data for the current state (you may think you know what is happening, but you will be surprised at how much you don't know)
2. Map current state—using the data from the interviews to create a process map
3. Evaluate tasks—analyze each task and determine if it is value-added (VA) or non-value added (NVA)
4. Brainstorm changes—all ideas are documented and the team decides which ones to implement
5. Develop future state—incorporate proposed short- and medium-term changes into the future state map.

Now the concept may be simple, but the group dynamics of each team is not. Once you get a group of people together, you need to make sure that each individual understands the role they play on the team. They may be an "expert" in the process, a "decision maker," a "novice" (someone new to the process), and a "support" person (someone who isn't directly involved with the process, but supports it—like an information systems [IS] person). The team members must also understand the scope of the process that is going to be mapped. Scope is such a big issue. You must have a start and an end; otherwise the team will flounder, go off on tangents, and not get anything accomplished.

## Rules Contribute to Success

Team members must also understand the rules for the events. We have some very basic rules that each team member must follow: Have an open mind; nothing is impossible; nothing is personal; nothing is sacred; we start on time, even after breaks; ask "why" five times; no side-bar conversations, and respect others' opinions.

We learned very early on to stress that "nothing is personal." People on the team and those individuals we bring in to interview need to understand that the interviewing process and the team questions are not personal. The individual happens to be the person who completes this particular part of the process. When the lean office concept became accepted by the employees and as more people began to participate in events, the "nothing is personal" rule has become part of the norm and we don't have to stress it as hard as we did in the beginning. We always make sure it is clearly understood during the training session at every event.

We have completed events for accounts payable, MRO receiving, new product development for our scrapbook albums, the capital expense request process, Creative Memories International, product pricing, the artwork process, the Engineering Change Request process, master planning, to name a few. We have also used the process to help a new department that acquired functions from other departments to determine the scope and mission of the department and what each individual was accountable for.

## Wastes Uncovered

As we have completed the events, we have noticed that there are several wastes that are repeated over and over again. They include lack of awareness, lack of communication, poor process flow, no process owner, lack of training, and unnecessary e-mails, photocopies, logs, etc.

## Lack of Awareness

Awareness has been our number one benefit from the lean office events. Awareness alone initiates change because people want to do the right thing. Once they understand the process, it allows them to maximize their potential.

Okay, so how have we achieved the infamous awareness? Awareness happens during the interviewing process and through general discussion throughout the event. Team members start to realize how they fit into the process as a whole and how their actions affect the up and down stream portions of the process. This is very powerful information. Team members also understand the frustrations and obstacles that other people deal with to make the process work. All of this information helps team members interact with empathy because they understand that each person is trying to do the right thing and not out to make their life miserable. We had teams from a few lean office events that felt the current process was fine and did not proceed to a future state (as facilitators you must be aware of the team's needs). In these cases we still had significant benefits due to awareness.

At Creative Memories we sell and ship many kits to our independent consultants. Kit contents change frequently and the changes are driven by new products that are offered. During the kit lean office event, one of the goals was to reduce the number of kit changes. During the event the team members from the sales department felt they had no control over the changes because marketing always introduces new products. At the first follow-up meeting the sales team members came forward with their action item results. Guess whose product changes were prompting all of the kit changes? The sales team! Now that they are aware of this situation and have direct control over these products, they will plan their product introductions according to when we want the kits to change instead of the other way around. We expect to see a significant decrease in the number of kit changes within six months.

## Lack of Communication

Lack of communication is a classic issue in any process. How many times have you had a problem with your portion of the process and worked out a solution without working with the individual before you in the process and after you in the process? This is very common in any office or production environment. We tend to add "Band-Aids®" to the process rather than working out the solution for the problem.

During our international department event, we found that the international department was doing an immense amount of paperwork chasing the U.S. market changes in product development. Each group was doing its own thing. The U.S. market marketing team was developing product, making changes when necessary, and launching the product. The international team would watch the engineering change request report to notice any changes to the product and then submit the appropriate paperwork for the international version of the product. In most cases, the only thing different between the U.S. product and the international version was the packaging.

After mapping out the process, we found that the process wasn't that bad, but rather the two groups were communicating poorly. One of the solutions was to add a monthly meeting, affectionately called the GI (good intentions) meeting, where the U.S. market and international market teams meet to discuss the U.S. new product plan. It also gives the international team the advance notice needed to determine if the international markets will add the product to their product line.

Besides improving communication, we have also saved money by having the international team involved in the new product development process early enough to suggest changes to the new product that would make the product universal for the markets.

**Figure 2.** International lean event participants shown from left to right are: Pui Hong Ang, Joan Edvenson, Stacy Blonigen, Mandy Sugget, Shanta Hendrickson, Bev Messer, Lynn Kelzenberg, Monica Schifsky, Deann Elfering, and Deb Eisenschenk.

## Poor Process Flow

Everyone knows what poor process flow is, but do you know where it is and how to fix it? Well, during our lean office event regarding engineering changes, it was very clear we had poor process flow. In this case, rework and communication loops were mapped in several areas.

It is easy to identify poor process flow when you physically can see it on a map. Just like when you are using a map to select a driving route—would you plan to stop at specific gas stations for directions and retrace your steps to get back on track? No! With that in mind we set our future state to be a straight line (as straight as possible) and eliminate the backtracking. The first communication loop we found was when paperwork was submitted with incomplete information, engineering services would attempt to process the information and then realize they did not have enough information. So, 10 or 15 minutes into it they had to stop and call the paperwork originator for more details. If the required information was not readily available, they had to file the paperwork in an on-hold folder and move on to the next request. When the information was available or when they checked their on-hold folder to follow up on old requests, they would familiarize themselves with the request again and attempt to process it. Sometimes they would run into another area requiring more information and the cycle would start all over again. Further down in the process, the map showed where product information was being finalized. This information was the missing detail in the initial paperwork submitted. We were astounded.

So what changed? The paperwork forms changed to clearly identify what information was required and we moved the product information to be finalized before submitting paperwork. When engineering services opens the request, they can visually scan to see if all the required information is available. If not, they send it back. Before this was implemented we trained all paperwork originators of the new process. Rework is down considerably.

## No Process Owner

How could a process not have an owner? It seems incredible but with the growth we have had, that question comes up during many of our lean office events. In some cases this question became an action item because it wasn't immediately clear within the team. All processes without owners have problems and they are not easy to change or fix until an owner is determined. To effectively hold a lean office event we now ensure there is an owner before scheduling an event.

During our system pricing event we mapped how product prices were entered into our computer system. We held the event due to an unacceptable number of pricing errors every month. Other key issues exposed during the event included different file formats, information not available in a timely manner, and our customers were affected by incorrect pricing.

As a result of the event, a process owner was defined, responsibilities were shifted, file formats were standardized, shared files were created, and timelines were put in place. The responsibilities to enter the price into the computer system and test the system to endure accuracy were moved to engineering services. The tasks were in line with the function of the department and since the department entered the majority of the system data, it made sense to give them the responsibility of system testing.

System pricing errors only accounted for ten percent of all system errors each month. Since moving and maximizing the testing function, total system errors have been reduced by 90 percent. Each pricing error costs $140. So we saved $7,500 annually for pricing errors. But since the testing was expanded beyond system pricing, the total savings for all system errors is $66,525 annually!

## Lack of Training

Training is a very hot topic. Companies spend millions of dollars each year training their employees. How do you really know if people are trained and if they are retaining what they have learned?

This was a very valuable lesson learned during our artwork lean event. The event's focus was to look at the development of a sticker pack from the conceptual state to the introduction stage. We spent several painful hours mapping the process to have the team agree that the process wasn't broken and they didn't need to go to the future state. The only problem was we had 124 action items—the most action items we ever had for a lean event. Something was obviously wrong.

After sorting out the action items, we found that many of them pertained to the lack of training with the new product developers. Everyone assumed that the new product developers were trained and followed the same processes. This was not the case. The solution to this issue: A team developed 13 one-hour training sessions. It took four weeks from the time the training issue was exposed to the time the training sessions started.

The results of the training have been phenomenal. Many of the other action items on the list were resolved by just training the individuals. One major issue was the artwork proofing process. A training session was dedicated to the proofing process. As of our last follow-up meeting with the team, we have gone from four-five proofing cycles to an average of three. Besides saving money for the company, it also reduces the leadtime of product development.

## Unnecessary e-mails, Photocopies, Logs, etc.

How many times have you received e-mail that you automatically deleted without reading, but never notified the sender you want to be removed from the distribution list? Have you ever asked yourself why you make a photocopy or why you print out e-mails? These are some wastes that can be eliminated easily if you just take the time to evaluate them.

During a lean office event, if writing and sending an e-mail is an activity, we always ask if the individuals on the distribution list are the appropriate individuals who need the information and we ask if the information being sent is being used. These questions need to be asked. Sending information that isn't being used or is incomplete is a waste of time along with sending the e-mail to an individual who doesn't belong on the distribution list.

During our lean office event with the accounts payable group, we were able to highlight several wastes in regards to photocopies, filing, and stapling. In the interviewing process, we found out that the accounts payable clerks were photocopying every check and direct deposit that was processed. They then stapled the copy of the check or direct deposit slip to the invoice or expense report. After asking why a few times, we found out that they were not only stapling the documents together, but they were stapling the documents twice. This was a habit formed from an old filing system that they had changed several years ago.

The controller challenged the clerks as to why we had to make a copy of every check and direct deposit slip. It was the way they had always done it. The group met with IS and had a report developed that listed all the checks and direct deposits for each check run. The report, the invoices, and expense reports are now filed by the date of the check run.

With these few simple changes—no copying and no stapling and virtually no filing—the accounts payable team saved eight hours a week. The copying and stapling were the least-liked task by the group. By eliminating them, the morale also increased within the team.

## What's Next

With the acceptance of the Lean Office Events at The Antioch Company, we started a new Lean Office Department in January 2003. The department consists of the two lean office co-founders or creators, a lean office manager, a facilitator, and an assistant. The lean office manager and facilitator are full time while the two co-founders spend about 25 percent of their time working on the concept and strategies of the department. The goal for 2003 is to complete two events per month, hold timely follow-up meetings with each team until the future state map has been met, develop a method to calculate intangible benefits in dollars, and launch a 6S program in the office.[2]

*Jane•Mobilia-Witte is the senior materials manager for The Antioch Company. She earned a B.A. degree in mathematics and an M.B.A. degree emphasizing operations management from St. Cloud State University. Her continuing education efforts include American Production and Inventory Control Society*

*(APICS) certification in production and inventory management, Institute for Supply Management certification in purchasing management, and she is a member of AME.*

*Kristi Huls is the engineering services manager for The Antioch Company. She earned a B.S. degree in engineering technology with a manufacturing emphasis from St. Cloud State University. She is a member of AME and APICS.*

## Footnotes

1.   The Antioch Company owns the business divisions of Antioch Publishing, Creative Memories, and zeBlooms. The company has four manufacturing facilities: St. Cloud, MN; Richmond, VA; and Sparks, NV operations manufacture albums for Creative Memories, while the Yellow Springs, OH facility manufactures stickers and other printed items for Creative Memories and bookmarks, journals, and a variety of other products for Antioch Publishing. The Sparks, NV facility distributes the zeBlooms line.
2.   The 6S program was launched in the office in May. The 6Ss includes sort, set in order, shine, safety, standardize, and sustain. This program evaluates storage, file retention, shared materials, ergonomics, and office supply stashes. It includes a point system for each team and points can be redeemed for organizational supplies.

## Questions

Are your employees involved in development of lean initiatives?

Does every person understand the role they play on the team and the rules for events?

Is every person aware of their role in your processes?

Is there good communication between employees and between groups in your organization?

Are you aware of points of poor process flow in your organization?

Does each of your processes have an owner?

Does every employee receive proper training?

Do employees produce unnecessary emails, photocopies, etc.?

# 5

# Lean Success in an Administrative Environment

Customer demand is the heart of the office, supported by a one-team philosophy.

*Mick Corrie*

---

**In Brief**

Initial success in Waukesha Bearings' administrative areas indicates that lean can be applied wherever there are customers and a process to serve them, according to author Mick Corrie. Centralized office workflow puts customer demand at the heart of the process.

---

Does lean translate to administrative areas? Our experiences at Waukesha Bearings Ltd. put this question to the test, specifically within our sales and engineering office headquartered in Northwood Hills on the outskirts of London. The company is a subsidiary of Dover Diversified Corporation and Dover Corporation (NYSE:DOV), a specialist engineering company that designs and manufactures bearings. Our products are tailored to meet customer needs in a variety of rotating machinery applications for power generation, oil/gas, chemical, and industrial use. Our lean journey began in November 2001 when George Koenigsaecker (chairman of the Shingo Prize), visited our executive team to discuss the potential of a "lean conversion."

The UK operation had been recently acquired by Dover, so this inaugural welcome to "lean thinking" was also a chance to meet with new colleagues from all of the corporation's bearing manufacturing sites. Each location sent representatives from human resources (HR), finance, production, engineering, sales, and operations to the event. We listened to the benefits of the whole enterprise "true conversion" to lean. As engineers, we accepted the relevance of lean for production yet questioned how lean could work in our engineering/administrative environment. In production , the formation of manufacturing cells and the development of takt time-driven standard work would obviously improve performance, but our non-manufacturing processes did not repeat and often the flow was different every time.

In sales and engineering, we signed up for a ten percent share of the 100 "rapid improvement events" to be run by Waukesha during 2002. We were soon to discover that lean would make a significant contribution across all areas, a dramatic transition from a traditional functional sales and engineering office.

## Slow Out of the Blocks

As predicted, the value stream mapping (VSM) process undertaken by our manufacturing colleagues went fairly smoothly. The input and output of manufacturing steps was relatively easy to identify, the scope being from the launch of an order and initial material release, right through to eventual packaging and dispatch. The goal of the "future state" map was to combine all of these steps into a single manufacturing cell, so that product could flow unhindered by waste. We realized this future state over a year by making huge changes to the way we did things and the benefits as a company have been tremendous.

The culture in our sales/engineering office was a little different in that the case for change seemed less compelling. We already prided ourselves on our relationships with customers and our applications engineering expertise. We were skeptical, to say the least. "How could lean help improve the performance of our office?" we asked Simpler Consulting people (who were helping us with our lean conversion). "There are so many different processes that take place within account management; lean will simply not be able to help us." We were pressed to list these processes. The first step was to map the key processes. Our fear was that to VSM just one of these processes would negate the value of all the other processes we do. In hindsight, we just needed to map one process to see what waste we had (the initial map is shown in Figure 1).

## The Three-Day Value Stream Mapping Events

Within our initial VSM event, we came to realize that many of the "different processes we do" were actually just pieces of a common value

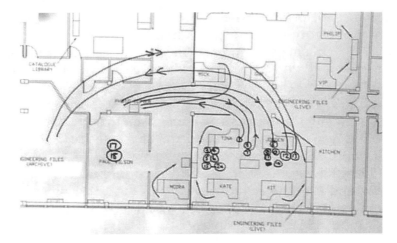

**Figure 1.** Distance traveled by a new inquiry (initial map).

stream. We also found that a major reason for a lot of both perceived (and real) variation was that there was no "current best way" shared by the team. In fact, almost all of our process steps were dependent on the individual style of the person doing the work. We were assured that this is normal in modern offices where most people work alone with their computer in a cubicle, rarely sharing process knowledge or improvement ideas that lead to action.

Our first value stream map defined, with absolute simplicity, the process behind our very existence: "To win profitable business for the company." This is what we do to add value. By looking at each step in the process, we learned that if we have process steps that don't contribute to this value, then we should really question, "Why do we do them?" Put even more simplistically, why does any company want processes that waste resources, including people's time, that do not contribute to the overall health of the company? It is easy to say, looking back, that our initial doubts about how lean could apply to us were natural and typical when you do not really understand lean fundamentals or practical realities of a lean conversion. Translate that doubt to denial of the change itself. It is a hard question to ask of anyone: "So how do you add value?" Asking yourselves is harder still.

The process we initially mapped was "the inquiry process" because it touched most individuals in our office and is really the first contact a customer has with our organization. Inquiries range from simple needs, such as a straight repeat order, to highly complex, one-off engineered solutions. For the mapping, our first "lean event" involved a cross-functional team of six people including myself as the team leader and, interestingly, a colleague from our manufacturing division. The neutrality of this team member and the consultant helped to keep the mapping process flowing as sales and engineering team members discussed and mutually agreed what the inquiry process steps were. The "outsiders" were great, as they could ask all the basic questions like, "Why? How? What for?" We discovered truly amazing variability in our process steps. Another finding: Mapping cannot be done in a conference room. You have to actually go, see, and touch the work to understand how it is really done.

Within 48 hours, we had created the current state map, an ideal state map, and finally a future state map. This last map was a statement of intent of what we wanted our inquiry process to be like within 6 to 12 months. The mapping process is labor intensive, but it took the team to such a deeper level of understanding of what was actually happening and that the case for change was compelling. For instance, we previously sensed that our response time on proposals to customers could be improved but was basically good. It was only when actual calendar time and touch times (worked on time) were determined that it brought home to us how much waste we actually had (it was substantial). Recording (with reluctance) actual times with stopwatches was a real culture shock. Reality never matches your hunches or theoretical times.

From the VSM project, it was clear that inquiries for repeat parts should be fast-tracked with less engineering support. Not only would this reduce the number of steps on repeat inquiries, but also enable engineering to focus on the value-adding steps required of new-engineered inquiries. In effect, the fast flow required for "repeats" was being held back by the other inquiries. Any individual could prioritize, stop, or re-sequence any job as they chose, compounding this effect. When you add the phone calls and interruptions, which are a normal part of any office life, it was easy to see why things took so long. So two future state VSMs were created, corresponding to "repeat" and "new" inquiries.

Customer value, in terms of inquiry response time, was now quantifiable from the future state map targeting one hour for repeat inquiries and one day for new inquiries. Through mapping, we had identified "our" waste—catalyst for real change. Change agents who recognized the opportunities of banishing waste once and for all emerged from both our sales and engineering departments, expressing a desire to "give it a go." We looked forward to our first rapid improvement event.

## Not Quite a Showcase

The lean movement went into overdrive with full backing from the top, especially at the manufacturing plants. We had to wait three months for our "sensei" (Chris Cooper of Simpler) to conduct our first rapid improvement event in the sales/engineering office. The unsightly current, future, and ideal state maps had remained on the walls all this time. After looking at these maps every day, we wanted to learn how to remove waste from our processes and we had identified the inquiry process as the main artery of the office, affecting sales and engineering personnel alike.

We set out in our first rapid improvement event to make a significant change in only five days. A new cross-functional team of six people (an account manager, three engineers, an estimator, and a customer service representative) was assembled, including two from the original team (creator of the value stream maps). The other four members had heard only an introductory presentation about lean concepts.

To ensure continuity of thinking and purpose, the team conducted a detailed analysis of the current inquiry process. We assessed each step of the existing process, noting the time it took, the distance traveled, whether the step added value (or not), and whether it could be done right the first time. The results revealed a close correlation to the data from the current state map, but the added detail allowed the team to set further targets for reduction in process steps, distance traveled, and work in progress.

In spite of these clear targets, change is never obvious until it is discovered. The team found it difficult to imagine a future state that was significantly different from the current desk-based environment. Breakthroughs occurred when Chris led the team out of the conference room and encouraged us to "trystorm" in the open office rather than "brainstorm." To reduce the effect of interruptions and reduce distance traveled between steps, we imagined a dedicated cell for the handling of inquiries.

A suitable location was identified, but again difficulties arose as time was taken up by the natural tendency to "brainstorm" and "intellectualize" our ideas. After a rapid series of "trystorming" activities in quick succession, the inquiry cell layout emerged. It was constructed four different ways before the team found a truly viable solution. The result, though, was a high-quality admin cell created in only five days. It could handle multiple customers/languages/currencies and products passing through it.

As we calculated the reduction in distance traveled by a repeat inquiry from 128 to 36 meters, an enduring lesson was learned: It is better to remove huge wasteful steps rather than slightly improve the value-added steps.

It is equally important to think way beyond today's traditional office layouts. If you think it through, most human-based processes add value when people collaborate, discuss, and make value-adding decisions. So why are 99 percent of the people in 99 percent of the offices in the world staring into computers in the corner of a cubicle? We learned to be wary of the "postponed perfection" that brainstorming often leads to when you literally talk your way out of doing anything. We learned to adopt a practical, step-by-step "try it then improve it" approach, which lifts morale as tangible improvements are made. Rather than just talk about things as we had done for years, we were changing things for the better.

The team gave a summary each evening to the rest of the office. This provided focus towards achieving things at the end of each day and we received good feedback and input.

As we ended the event, a whiteboard (one of many disused items located) was commandeered to enable everyone to give "safe" feedback without judgment beyond the event itself. The same whiteboard was also utilized to make visual the number of inquiries in/out each day, marking our first step towards performance measurement in an admin environment.

## One Step Back

Within two weeks of creating the admin cell, the task of flowing inquiries through the cell had become intolerable to those using it. In our office different skills are mixed to handle a number of inquiries concurrently; the cell had, in fact, become an inhibitor to flow. We saw graphically that our customer demand was random; it seemed every time a new inquiry arrived, the cell was already occupied (picture the scene of people jostling for position to use the cell). This problem resulted in regular batching-and-queuing of work at the entrance to the cell. With time ticking on the response times for these inquiries, people quickly returned to personal desks to complete the work. Conversely, there would also be times when no one was using the cell. In our minds we had effectively created a cell, which was at times too small for the number of people required to operate it and at other times too big. We did learn that the perceived issue of "interruptions," which led to the creation of a stand-alone cell, was not as big a problem as we had thought.

Needless to say, our production board (whiteboard) was quickly packed with ideas and suggestions, and it was the richness of their feedback that directed our next rapid improvement event. The original intention was to conduct a 6S (sort out, straighten, scrub, standardize, sustain, and safety) event for the whole office, but the rate of issues arising from the cell outstripped our ability to resolve them. We felt we had reached a crossroads with lean. Feelings were mixed. The cell had had an adverse effect on our response times but mapping the inquiry process had been successful in identifying waste to banish.

On his return Chris Cooper smiled and asked us, "What has the cell revealed?" He encouraged us to think of improvements to build on what our cell had taught us. It was at this precise moment that top management (the ultimate sponsor) truly began to devolve responsibility for improvements and placed trust in the decisions being taken at a local level. It would have been all too easy to identify another process to "lean" and report positive results upwards, but if the local team were to remain enthusiastic, we needed to find a solution to the difficulties we were experiencing. We received full backing to re-look at the cell, which to the unenlightened could look like a duplication of the earlier five-day event. This event week was to become a pivotal point for sustainable success.

## Two Steps Forward

A second cross-functional team was formed for the event. From our previous teachings we recruited two neutrals representing manufacturing and IT. It is now our tradition to actively change and mix team players so that everyone gets an equal opportunity to participate and we have the right skills available as needed. The numerous issues concerning the admin cell fell into many categories and provoked a variety of opinion. We were shown the cause and effect problem-solving tool which quickly lent itself to the separation of opinions from facts. Our understanding was strengthened by a series of interviews of all cell users. The main problem causes were soon identified and solutions sought.

Rather refreshingly, the admin cell was deemed not to be quite the failure we had believed it to be. It had actually been very successful in revealing underlying issues. Small islands of excellence, such as some impromptu sharing of engineering workload on new inquiries and visual performance measurement, had come to light through its execution. We did not want to lose these benefits.

The team decided that their plan of action for this event would be how to make the workload leveling process happen office-wide. We were assured that initial cells always reveal underlying issues to be solved, so the cell had indeed done its job. We had learned that although individuals had in-trays and phones, we needed to think of the whole office as having a collective in-tray that could, and should, be processed differently from the typical, ever-changing feast and famine of one person as ultra-busy, the next person, not.

So the team constructed a workflow control system in the middle of the office. A "visual" place was needed and real success would only come if it were easy to get in and operate. Intense "trystorming" ensued which now engrossed most of the office. Out went 11 partitions, four tables, two desks, and 17 boxes of paperwork, which could be archived. This freed up floor space so that printers and fax machines, which had been sitting in passageways, could be relocated to an ideal true point of use (see Figure 2).

**Figure 2.** Achieving line of sight visibility across the office.

This process of simplifying the physical office layout had a wide-reaching effect on everyone involved in the inquiry process. Personal desks were moved and separate filing systems, which had evolved in different quarters of the office, were co-located with a standardized method of file storage and retrieval agreed among all parties.

The most profound impact to the working environment was yet to come—climbing over the psychological hurdle of losing personal in-trays from one's desk to the new centralized office workflow system. This change was necessary to achieve a visual process for the entire office. The positive benefits of the cell were retained and re-integrated onto people's desks, whilst solving one of the main obstacles to fast flow (smoothing and leveling the load).

## Concurrent One-Piece Flow

Whilst it may have been difficult in its execution, the centralized office workflow system has paid enormous dividends by placing customer demand at the heart of the process. It is analogous to a customer standing in the middle of an office pulling the whole team along.

Over the past several months since we have been operating our new lean system, average response time on inquiries (repeat and new combined) decreased from 5.6 days to 1.3 days. This improvement enables us to work up the monthly number of inquiries received in to buck the current downturn in our markets and use freed-up time to do sales, stimulating follow-up calls that we previously didn't have the time to do.

We use one-piece flow so that no individual works on more than one inquiry at a time. For that reason, new inquiries are placed directly into the workflow system to minimize the disturbances to flow that were previously attributed to an open plan office. Actually the real disturbance was the natural tendency to "take a quick look at it to see what it is." Work no longer gathers on personal desks, eliminating the flow-destroying batch-and-queue. All "live" inquiries are transparent on the desks and the level of work in progress/incoming is visible for the whole office in the central workflow system (see Figure 3).

Are you wondering how you will know when to offer assistance if you can't see your neighbors' workload? Doing this with personal in-trays would mean walking around the office and asking (disturbing) questions—no longer needed with our new workflow system. We have proven to ourselves that agile customer service can be achieved when a team is prepared to share and level the workload. In essence,

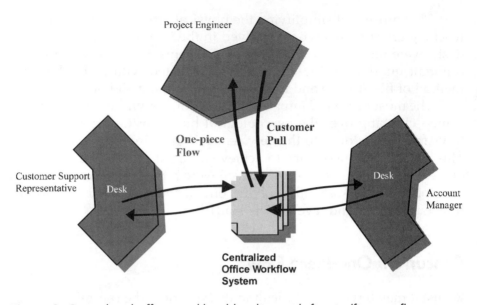

**Figure 3.** Centralized office workload leveling with first in/first out flow system (FIFO).

our sales/engineering has become a closer team which is self-managing and responsive to the rate of customer demand. The traditional "hot list" and crisis management that traditionally dominated the office is no longer employed.

A strange calmness has arrived. The leadership role has changed from direct management and trying to work out what the performance level was at any time to that of coaching and developing best practices with the team. If, for whatever reason, it is not possible to achieve a desired result, then we look at the process first. There have been examples where we found our new process steps were not explicit enough, prompting improvement of our standard work instructions which underpin our new lean methods.

## Keeping the Habit

Our production board, which previously buckled under the weight of issues, was also moved to a central location. We quickly recognized that the new office workflow system would not be the "issues monster" that the dedicated admin cell had been. We were relieved that the *quality* of event result had been placed above number of events in our new approach; now we could look forward to new events.

| Before Lean | After Lean |
|---|---|
| Batch-and-queue on desks | Visible work in progress across office |
| Partitioning/cubicles | Line of sight visibility |
| Uneven workloads | Level workload (shared) |
| Fire fighting | Calm |
| Group working | Team working |
| 5.6 days to respond | 1.3 days or less |
| Unknown performance | Performance and targets |
| 'Hot-list' management | Self management |

**Figure 4.** Comparison of "before" and "after" lean conversion.

As ideas appeared on the production board, we formed a multi-functional team representing sales and production, meeting monthly to work out how best to address them. Minutes are issued with tasks assigned and deadlines set to ensure successful implementation. We avoid repeating ourselves by capturing all ideas in a "to do list" before the production board is wiped clean for the next month.

There is no better motivator to idea stimulation and improvement than actually providing regular time for it. It was through this process that we targeted the need to improve our next key process: creating an order. Again, this is a process requiring a lean enterprise approach between sales and engineering to translate customer requirements efficiently.

Lean has taught us that, put bluntly, every day in admin is one day less to manufacture the goods. So with the benefit of our firmly established workflow system and our experience in lean and teamwork growing, our next event ran smoothly. The workflow system was upgraded and modified to incorporate the order-taking process, enabling us to extend one-piece flow across two key processes. We have subsequently used lean tools to improve many aspects of our work, changing our culture.

## Conclusion

It is important to think far beyond today's office layouts, methods, and approaches. Using external advice and building on our existing skills/experience, we learned to apply lean in non-traditional areas. Our commitment to lean conversion must be long-term for our success to be maintained. Having completed more than 100 lean events in

2002, we continued to extend lean process improvements during 2003 by realizing a similar number of dedicated lean events.

In our sales and engineering office, we have achieved a one-team philosophy, encouraging knowledge-sharing and development within an open climate. Improvement ideas continue to be added to our production board, underlining the fact that the removal of waste never ends. To banish waste, the process needs to be visible to everyone. Lean has had a dramatic and positive impact on our ability to provide customers with a competitive service.

Since the implementation of our lean inquiry/order workload system, we have underpinned our lean conversion with an office-wide 6S event, scoring 96 percent in our audit. In turn, we created "free" floor space, decreasing our original footprint by 50 percent. We will revisit our future state map annually as we set more ambitious targets and we will continue to place customers as the primary pull for all of our processes. We feel we are only at the beginning of our journey of possibilities with lean: improving yield, minimizing backflows, avoiding rework, sharing best practices (internally and externally), developing lean enterprise thinking in collaboration with suppliers and customers. Our initial success proves that lean can be applied wherever there are customers and a process to serve them.

*Mick Corrie, business team manager, Waukesha Bearings Ltd., Northwood Hills, UK (www.waukbearing.com).*

---

## Questions

Do you have a "current best way" for each process?

Does each of your teams include at least one "outsider" who is not part of the process being reviewed?

Do your teams "trystorm" outside the conference room?

Do you follow a "try it, then improve it" approach?

Has a first attempt at improvement ever failed to work the way you anticipated? What did you do as a result?

Have you ever tried to simplify office layouts? Have you eliminated personal in-boxes?

Have you tried to achieve one-piece flow in office processes?

# 6

# Lean Office: Mapping Your Way to Change

Learning to eliminate non-value-added activities in the office.

*Lea A.P. Tonkin*

## In Brief

Learning to eliminate non-value-added (NVA) activities in office processes can be challenging. This article offers "how to" information for getting started on lean office events and related "lessons learned" at The Antioch Company.

Now that you've "leaned" the way you do things in your production areas, what's next? Sure, continuous improvement will bring added results to the shop over time. But what about your office areas — the administrative types, the sales and marketing people, not to mention legal, engineering, and others? Participants in an AME workshop in St. Cloud, MN, "Lean Office Events — Mapping Your Way to Change,"[1] learned how to apply lean principles in non-production areas. The event included a kaizen blitz, presentation, and plant tour at The Antioch Company in St. Cloud.

## Awareness: Need for Change

Sometimes there's a reluctance to acknowledge the need for lean outside of the production floor. Before launching an attack on waste in office processes, you need to determine what bottlenecks cost time and money (not to mention frustration) in day-to-day activities, said Kristi Huls, president of Successflo, a training group within Antioch. She and

Successflo Vice President Jane Mobilia-Witte facilitated the workshop.

Mobilia-Witte suggested that, if you answer "yes" to any of these questions, you should consider implementing a lean program in your office:

1. Is overtime common?
2. Is rework a fact of life?
3. Do employees spend a lot of time compiling, copying, and filing paperwork?
4. Is there more than one way to perform a task? Is one way better than another?
5. Do employees spend time searching for files, messages, or packages?
6. Has the company grown without changing processes?
7. Have Band-aids® been applied to areas that were broken?

Conversely, a "no" answer to the following questions can prompt consideration of a lean office program:

1. Do you have standardized procedures?
2. Do you implement best practices?
3. Does every process have an owner?
4. Do employees understand how their role affects a process?
5. Do people communicate the right information at the right time to the right people?

Going lean in the office isn't easy. In the shop, employees may be accustomed to increasing productivity and efficiency. In the office, some people do not know what productivity is and they may not have heard of lean. "I recall two things vividly when we first started lean events in our company," said Huls. "One, people thought it was a new employee named Lena Vent, and two, after we gave out shirts for each event that had the phrase 'Lean Event' on them, employees wearing the shirts were asked what weight loss program they belonged to. Many office employees may not have thought about whether their jobs and processes are efficient. Since they aren't part of the direct cost of the product, they are left behind on the journey to lean. But in fact, the office is where you'll find most of your opportunity; improving value-added here will eventually affect your organization's bottom line and hopefully your product cost."

Why is it so hard to bring lean concepts into the office? Among the numerous reasons cited by Mobilia-Witte and Huls are: no time, lack of understanding, lack of cooperation between departments, not a directive from the top (so why do it?), belief that lean does not work in the office, and an attitude that office workers are above that kind of program. The list can go on forever, they noted, and employees at each company have different reasons reflecting their culture.

## Analyze Metrics

Before you get started on a lean office event, consider metrics. Metrics must be analyzed during lean office events to ensure that they meet the needs of the project, and that results from the event can be documented. If you don't have a baseline to measure against, or don't know what should be measured, a lean office event is a means to develop appropriate metrics and generate action items where improvements are needed, according to Huls. She suggested starting on a small pilot, then moving to more complex projects.

"Metrics are a great way to see how you are performing. But do you know if you are measuring the right things or getting accurate information? For example, one of our plants showed excellent bill of material (BOM) and router accuracy," said Huls. "It turned out that the data we gathered had been staged after errors were found and fixed! Currently we take a sampling of products that were manufactured during the month and check the BOM and router for accuracy. We recently realized that when the sample run is produced, the BOM and router are checked by manufacturing and updated prior to full production. Guess what? Our accuracy for sample runs is not pretty. Were our metrics set up blindly? Absolutely not. We initially set them up in three of our facilities; they effectively reflect BOM and router accuracy. We transferred the metric to our fourth facility, which has different product lines and processes; the metric was useless at the fourth site.

"In another example, we worked with a company that builds and delivers construction equipment. During a lean office event, a customer pointed out that deliveries were always late. The manufacturer could not confirm or dispute the claim, because they were not measuring on-time delivery. After the metric was implemented, they rated 27 percent on-time delivery. The customer was right. Action items derived from the event focused on improving on-time delivery. Those systems were implemented, such as ensuring paperwork follows the machine from production through shipping, and also determining realistic ship dates in conjunction with the customer, marketing, engineering, and production. On-time delivery significantly improved."

## Updating Your Metrics

Metrics need tune-ups, too. Business practices change over time, and yesterday's yardsticks may no longer be appropriate.

"For years, we recorded the products that were returned to our company," said Mobilia-Witte. "It is important information for product design, quality engineering, marketing, sales, and shipping. We were surprised that we weren't showing improvements in this area based on efforts to improve the products that rated high for returns. That is because one of the products being tracked was not really a product. It was a marketing tool that we mailed monthly to all company representatives. If it was undeliverable, it showed as a return. But, in reality, this tool was never really returned. This mailing, sent to 70,000 people, had a considerable undeliverable rate. In fact, the variety and number of mailed pieces has increased substantially over the last few years. The solution was to set up an additional metric specifically for mailed pieces to drill down and localize our undeliverable issues. After a new metric was implemented, the returns metric finally reflected our product improvement efforts. Returns went from .3 percent to .1 percent. The mailing metric now provides enough information to take action for improvement."

Metrics can drive the wrong behavior, added Huls. She said, "We kept a spreadsheet showing the milestone status for all product development projects. During a recent lean office event, we found that this spreadsheet was a great tool for some, but wreaked havoc for many others. In order to maintain a good status on milestones, project managers were massaging the dates. The metric drove them to change dates and timelines to make it look like a project was on track instead of working with the team to meet the milestones. This activity absorbed many hours every week. We deleted the milestone status from the spreadsheet and the project teams, not just the project leader, now are responsible for keeping their projects on track."

What do you do with your metrics? "If your metrics don't cause you to take action, then what is their purpose? During one of our lean office events, a team member asked what we did with the information gathered about the sources of engineering changes," continued Huls. "The intent was to work with the departments that submitted the most unplanned changes. Guess what? Follow-up discussions to eliminate the excessive engineering changes did not take place. It also turned out that the information about engineering changes is readily available as a computer report that can be pulled anytime. When the need arises to

## Twelve Steps of a Lean Office Event

1. Prepare. Select the team, create the initial project scope and goals with the process owner, and coordinate the event.
2. Train the team. A little training goes a long way to ensure a successful event.
3. Finalize the scope and goals. Do this with team members during the event, setting boundaries and the tone for the next couple of days.
4. Document the high-level process outline. This breaks down the process into usable sections for the interviewing process.
5. Interview team members in the process. Gather details about the current state and capture action items and ideas.
6. Create a current state map.
7. Define the value-added activities. Emphasize that only five to ten percent of activities will be value-added in many projects.
8. Develop the future state map.
9. Review and assign action items and assign responsibility.
10. Recap what transpired during the event, celebrate, and close — time to send the team off to work on action items!
11. Post-event activities. Put all of the information documented throughout the event into an electronic format and share it with the team, and make it accessible to others in the organization through the company intranet or other means.
12. Follow-up meetings; reconvene one to two months after the event and review the status of the planned changes. Up to four follow-up sessions are typically needed before the future state is fully implemented.

analyze the information, we can run the report and take action. The metric was abolished."

Huls and Mobilia-Witte noted that metrics should tie to the bottom line. "This is doable with the right metrics," Huls said. "But how do you put a dollar value on communication? Our biggest benefit from a lean office event is awareness among team members. When they leave the event, they all understand the up- and downstream parts of their process. It's a way to remedy the common situation in which team members don't know each other and how their activities affect others' activities, even though they are part of the same process. During the event, people get to know each other and they develop a bond. In turn, once they leave the event, their day-to-day communication improves. When their communication improves, what impact can that have on the bottom line? Perhaps it will result in reduced rework, quicker turn-around time, or higher-quality products." Huls noted a continuing challenge is how to quantify those performance gains and link them with overall organizational performance, and that average annual savings resulting from each Antioch lean office event is $32,000.

## Getting Started

When Huls and Mobilia-Witte started the lean office program, it was a grassroots effort. Their motivation was simply to apply all of the lean concepts they had learned from various conferences, books, and seminars. "Getting started doesn't have to be complex or difficult," they said. "We believe our program is effective because it is simple, effective, and non-invasive."

Once you've documented the need to evaluate the activities in your office, where do you start? Huls and Mobilia-Witte said that the typical two-day lean office event process is fairly simple. (See the box, "Twelve Steps of a Lean Office Event.") Select the process (request process, accounts payable, etc.) you want to improve. "Just get started on a process that needs improvement rather than spending a lot of time researching how you can save the company a million dollars. Initially we all know what processes need an overhaul," Huls said. "Don't bite off more than you can chew on an initial project; you can expand to other processes later."

"We use facilitators to conduct our lean office events," said Mobilia-Witte. "They remain neutral, unbiased, and keep the team focused and on track. The facilitator develops the initial project scope, goals, and team roster with the process owner. It is important to involve them in planning the event."

The facilitator schedules and coordinates the event. Huls said that, during the event, the facilitator trains the team on lean office concepts, the techniques (such as defining value and developing a future state) they will use to analyze their process, and their roles. A clear understanding of roles played by individuals in the lean office event will enhance your project success. Process experts, novices, facilitators/support people, and decision makers all contribute to needed changes.

Following project "rules" can make or break the project. Huls and Mobilia-Witte are not advocating a stuffy, formal project. They'd like

## About Process Mapping

**First:** Gather information about the process current state, interviewing associates involved in the process. You may uncover some surprises about what's really happening.

**Second:** Map the process current state. Develop a process map based on the data collected in your initial interviews.

**Third:** Analyze the tasks you've documented. Are they NVA (non-value-added) or VA (value-added)?

**Fourth:** Brainstorm solutions/changes. Document these ideas. Then, as a team, select the one you will implement or schedule as an action item.

**Fifth:** Create a future state map. How should the process look in the near term, also medium-term, and long-term?

**Sixth:** Get started on the changes, measuring your performance against your goals.

people to have some fun while they're taking non-value-added activities (NVA) out of their processes. By rules, they mean: Be open-minded, don't take it personally, nothing is off limits within the process being evaluated, respect other team members' opinions, ask "why" five times to find the root causes of problems, start meetings on time, and don't hold side conversations during project discussions.

Although office work flows vary widely, there are common wastes uncovered during the lean projects. Among the NVA discoveries made most often during these events are: lack of awareness, poor communication, ineffective or jumbled process flow, multiple files with the same information, excessive photocopying, rework, etc.

The team finalizes the scope and goals for the event. It is important to define the scope. Mobilia-Witte said it's also useful to know the team members' objective in changing the process. Their answers usually highlight the "broken" areas of the process.

Next, develop a high-level "map" of the process, similar to an outline. (See the box, "About Process Mapping.") Interview associates working in the selected area to gain current state details. This is the time to find out what's really happening versus what you think is happening. Interviewing brings out unresolved issues and ideas for change, captured by the facilitator on a flip chart.

The team is dismissed after interviewing is complete. The facilitator creates the current state process map and then brings the team back together to review it.

Then the team is ready to create a future state process map. The whole team brainstorms ideas for change and determines what the future will look like. The facilitator creates the map as each part of the process is changed.

"It is now time to review all of the action ideas captured throughout the event," Huls said. "Assign accountability and due dates to the items that apply to the future state. Depending on the complexity of the action items, set a date for the first follow-up meeting. This usually happens 30–60 days after the event."

"A great example of outcomes emerged from an event regarding product artwork," said Mobilia-Witte. "A team reviewed the process from the time product artwork was requested through production. The artwork was always late and production was always squeezed for time. We found the process itself wasn't flawed, but our company had so many new people who had no idea what the process was. The team ended up with over 100 action items. Most of them were categorized as 'training gap issues.' A team was assigned to develop a training program. Six weeks later, a 13-workshop program was rolled out. Everyone associated with product development was required to attend. It was updated and presented each quarter for a year. The artwork process runs more smoothly and new hires learn the process via an assimilation program."

A process to coordinate conventions was analyzed in another event. "Our company holds an annual national convention for 10,000 representatives," Huls said. "It takes two years to plan and it touches every department in the company. This example illustrates the benefits of awareness. We recently held a follow-up meeting and changed the process again! One of the steps in the future state was to have a meeting to inform people about a specific aspect of the convention. This was put in place because key people were not aware of the process. Or more to the point, they were not aware of the up- and downstream effects of not following the process. Due to the lean office event and other process changes, the team was able to eliminate that informational meeting. Simply holding the event made people aware of certain issues (such as information required and the importance of keeping deadlines) and led to their resolution. These kinds of things are what prompted the tagline," Team Solutions, Priceless Knowledge."

**Figure 1.** Antioch team members brainstorming process changes.

## Sustaining

Follow-up meetings are critical. "Without these, not much will change," said Mobilia-Witte. "The facilitator coordinates and runs these meetings. Continue holding follow-up meetings until the future state is implemented. Work with the process owner to quantify the benefits of the changes. At the last meeting, update the future state map to reflect the actual changes and share the results with the team. Celebrate!"

Keep the improvement momentum going. Schedule lean events on a regular basis; share results with senior management and throughout the organization. Recognize lean project teams, and post results (and/or share on your company intranet, etc.). Fellow employees will understand what can be achieved in the lean events if they learn what the event was about and what was achieved — including ways that obstacles inhibiting performance were eliminated. Introduce lean concepts to new and current employees through training sessions, brochures, and other communications. All of these approaches depend on your company's culture.

Sharing results in whatever way you can spurs more lean activities throughout the company, according to Mobilia-Witte and Huls. Last year, after attending a lean event for the first time, an Antioch employee from the sales department applied the lean concepts to other aspects of her job. "She took the time to update a mailing list that had been used for years," said Huls. "This individual's effort saved our company $40,000 annually in mailing costs."

## Lessons Learned

Huls and Mobilia-Witte offered "lessons learned" suggestions for others embarking on lean office projects:
- Keep it simple
- Don't over-analyze
- Get started!

*Editor's note: Jane Mobilia-Witte and Kristi Huls co-authored the article "Lean Office Events — Priceless Knowledge, Team Solutions," in the Third Quarter 2003 issue of* Target.

*Lea A.P. Tonkin,* Target *editor, lives in Woodstock, IL.*

## Footnote

1.    Kristi Huls and Jane Mobilia-Witte of The Antioch Company will be presenters at the AME annual conference October 18-22 in Cincinnati; their topic will be Lean Office — Mapping Your Way to Change. The Antioch Company, based in Yellow Springs, OH owns the business divisions of Antioch Publishing, Creative Memories, zeBlooms, and Our Own Image. It has four manufacturing plants. Employees at facilities in St. Cloud, MN; Richmond, VA; and Sparks, NV make albums and pages and distribute product for Creative Memories; bookmarks, journals, and other products for Antioch Publishing; and distribute Our Own Image products. The Sparks, NV employees also distribute the zeBlooms line. Huls and Mobilia-Witte noted, "We have been doing lean office events for two years. As word got out about what we were doing, it generated many requests for more information. So, in 2003, Successflo™ was launched as a service of The Antioch Company. It includes a workshop to teach people how to facilitate a lean office event for their organization. Our mission is to provide premium programs and easy-to-use tools to help others create a lean office environment."

## Questions

Do your office employees understand what productivity is in their operations and how to measure it?

Do you have metrics for measuring office performance? Are they the right metrics?

Do you regularly follow up on measurements, using them as a basis for improvement actions?

Do facilitators conduct your office events?

Do you have project rules?

Do you schedule lean events on a regular basis?

Do you share results throughout the company?

# Elgin Sweeper Company Employees Clear a Path Toward Lean Operations with their Lean Enterprise System

Where 5S and lean events are part of the culture.

*Lea A.P. Tonkin*

**In Brief**

Elgin Sweeper Company employees learned how to do 5S right during the past few years, as lean concepts became part of their culture. Improvement projects in administrative, engineering, and sales areas as well as production work centers yielded significant initial performance improvements and "lessons learned;" the lean journey continues.

Within the past few years, people at Elgin Sweeper Company, Elgin, IL, literally cleaned up their act, discovered how to make employee involvement (EI) work well, and reaped the benefits of an enterprise-wide commitment to lean operations. Plant employees led the way in this cultural change, but process mapping and learning how to share information for improvement are concepts now at work in engineering, finance, sales, and other administrative areas.

Implementation results so far have been notable — cost savings, higher productivity, reduced space requirements enabling production to be brought in from another facility, etc. Next will come follow-up rounds for improvement blitzes — and keen attention to sustaining the gains over time, according to General Manager Tom White. Participants in an AME workshop, "5S Process and Tour" at Elgin Sweeper learned more about this success story.

# Elgin's Lean Enterprise System

As a market leader in the street sweeping equipment industry, you'd think Elgin Sweeper could've tolerated "the way things were." However, back in 1997, Mark Weber (currently group president, then serving as vice president of operations) realized that the potential for continued success depended on improving all areas of the enterprise. He initiated a Lean Steering Committee led by a lean coordinator (a lean expert with experience in Toyota Production System [TPS]-type production systems), along with the plant manager, business managers, the materials manager, and two manufacturing engineering project leaders. The Lean Steering Committee meets twice a week to keep the lean momentum strong, develop strategies, charter projects and resources and monitor lean implementation efforts.

At the start of the lean journey, most of the manufacturing operations were arranged in a typical batch process. The first lean pilot project was to create a weld cell to manufacture hydraulic tanks. This cell also piloted Elgin's pull systems strategy. The results were astounding; quality improved and shortages of hydraulic tanks disappeared overnight. After several more successful pilots, process/product mapping was used to identify new layouts for the entire manufacturing and assembly processes. The 5S (Sort, Set in Order, Shine, Standardize,

---

### About Elgin Sweeper

The company's sweepers have been cleaning roadways for many years. John Murphy of Elgin, IL noted the dusty, muddy condition of area roads, and invented a machine to pick up debris and collect it in a front hopper. The first sweeper was delivered to Boise, ID in 1914. Murphy's three-wheel design allowed the machine operator to maneuver around carriages, horses, and automobiles.

The Elgin Sweeper name means exceptional sweeping performance and longevity, according to the company. Whether the need calls for broom, vacuum, or regenerative air; ground-dump or variable height dump; general street maintenance, specialty airport, PM10 efficient, waterless, or alternative fuel vehicle — there is an Elgin Sweeper model to fit the application. As part of the Federal Signal Environmental Products Group, the company continues to add new, specialized products. Just as important is the company's network of more than 80 dealers worldwide who provide customers with service, training, and parts availability.

Sustain) process was then utilized over a two-year period in the implementation of the new layout on a cell by cell basis.

A key element of Elgin Sweeper's 5S program is that it was incorporated in a "blitz" format based on training received from an AME 5S Blitz held at the company several years ago. The entire 5S process is accomplished in a targeted work area during a two- to-three-day focused blitz. According to Jeanne Hem, former lean coordinator, this approach created an opportunity for complete participation with the operators in the targeted work area so they could totally focus on layout and improvement opportunities in a team setting. As the blitzes rolled out across the plant over three years, cultural change emerged. The workforce gained greater involvement and understanding of lean. The 5S process also facilitated necessary layout changes to move the plant from batch processing to cells and implement pull systems plant-wide.

The radical cultural change accompanying this "lean sweep" could hardly be underestimated. Employees learned how to take a new look at the traditional ways they'd worked for years, then swap ideas with fellow employees about better ways to do their work, and then made good ideas happen. They changed layouts, eliminated paperwork, shared ideas with each other on a regular basis, and figured out ways to trim waste as they made jobs easier. Plant employees previously worked in their specialty as welders or assemblers, etc. but now are being trained to work in cross-functional areas.

This 5S/lean campaign (Elgin Sweeper dubbed its program Lean Enterprise System, or LES) does not mean unfocused "Let's change something around here!" activities. It is a disciplined approach that asks employees to be accountable for their results. Elements of the company's 5S blitz process are shown in Figure l.

## How the 5S Events Work

Elgin Sweeper's initial plan to use 5S events in all areas of the operation, from the plant floor to engineering, finance, and other areas of the business was geared towards streamlining work areas, explained General Manager Tom White. "Though it initially served as a lever for culture change by introducing lean into the organization, most 5S project areas were initially selected according to business impact," he said. "Now they get the green light based on a combination of supervisor request and/or audit process scoring."

## Elgin Sweeper's 5S Blitz Process

- Identify the area for 5S improvements
- Select team members and identify their roles
- Develop and document a team charter (safety, quality, etc. improvements)
- Logistics
- Training in 5S and lean basics
- Set a budget
- Conduct the project
- Provide a 30-day list of action items not completed during the initial event with assigned responsibilities
- Senior management walk-around to see the improvements at work and hear about the project details, plus team recognition
- Audit process ("We stubbed our toe a few times until we learned that we need this step to follow up on the actual event," said Roger Himrod.)
- The team/management discuss learnings and pitfalls discovered during the event.

Figure 1.

## 5S Event Logistics Checklist

- Complete event charter
- Reserve meeting area
- Create an event folder — paper and electronic (create/use standard forms)
- Coordinate lunches and refreshments
- Take "before" photos
- Send event invitations
- Supplies — cleaning, paint, etc.
- Identify any known needed purchases in advance
- Coordinate resources — maintenance, suppliers, etc.
- Take "after" photos
- Schedule wrap-up team recognition.

Figure 2.

Every 5S blitz has a sponsor (a manager or supervisor) who sets goals, assembles the team, and attends daily updates to help clarify any issues as needed. The team also has a facilitator to coordinate project logistics, monitor team progress during the event, and challenge the team to push harder. The ideal facilitator is a veteran of such events, has served as a team leader in at least two 5S blitz events, and demonstrates lean leadership abilities. A team leader is appointed for every event to organize and lead team activities, as well as to keep the team on track. Qualifications for team leader include participation in at least two 5S blitz events, leadership skills, and the ability to work with team dynamics. The core 5S project team members are mostly area "owners." At least one "outsider" from other areas or functions is included. White noted that teams include three to ten members, depending on the area being evaluated and specific needs.

The team charter is critical to the blitz project success. It defines the area, date for the 5S blitz, process boundaries (start and end points), key objectives, and measures as well as the sponsor, facilitator, and team roster. Among the charter objectives for an engineering area 5S blitz, for example, were: Clean out and clean off all work areas; standardize work areas; develop visual measures and post for each group; organize the engineering library; provide access to departmental references, etc. The 5S project logistics basics cited by White are shown in Figure 2.

Corporate funding for 5S events has helped to build improvement momentum. Lighting, peg boards, work tables, paint tooling, and signage are among the items funded. However, 5S as a rule should not be cost prohibitive, according to White. He noted that for some events, the only outlays were for food. Advance planning of needed items for standardized work areas prevents extra expense and employees expecting extra gadgets, etc.

A 30-day checklist (called an Opportunity Log or Op Log) covers targeted improvement areas that have not been completed by the end of the 5S blitz event. One member is assigned to be in charge of following up on these items; the entire team discusses and ranks items for later action, limiting follow-up items that need outsourcing and indicating those requiring a capital expenditure.

# Training

Elgin Sweeper lean champions have learned that 5S and lean training is most useful when it is provided close to the time associates will begin using it. The plant lean coordinator developed separate shop and office 5S training packages, used at the start of the event. The team also receives lean training utilizing a Lego exercise in which teams of up to 12 participants simulate batch processing and one-piece flow.

The 5S training covers all the "Ss" and "Why we are doing this." For employees, it's discussed as a way to provide a safer and more pleasant workplace, creating ownership and a process that makes sense. For the company, 5S initiatives feed into overall lean objectives of better quality, less waste, and higher customer satisfaction, according to David Eakins, project manager and 5S facilitator.

Employees also learn about yellow tagging in the "Sort" training. Yellow tags are placed on unneeded equipment, supplies, etc. that should be removed from the work area. Items used daily can stay in the work area, items used weekly remain in the cell, those items used monthly stay in the plant, and anything not used in a year is thrown out. A "quick and ruthless" yellow tagging approach is suggested (being mindful of possible long-term needs for various kinds of tooling, etc.).

For the "Set in order" training, associates learn to arrange materials and other needed items so they are easily used. That means putting them where they can be quickly located, with correct (easy to read) labeling and documentation as needed. Visual controls indicate how work should be done; tool boards and color coding make it a challenge to put tools, etc. in the wrong place. Tool storage is based on frequency of use; tools used together are stored together. Developing a map of the work process flow, with arrows on a floor plan showing how things move along from one stage to the next, yields valuable information. Associates evaluate this "spaghetti diagram" and then draw a streamlined map of a more efficient work flow.

"Shine" activities are pretty much self explanatory. Get rid of grit and grime, maintain tools and equipment, and do some inspection of the work area and related tools and equipment. Develop a schedule for checking the work area and then cleaning/painting etc. as needed.

The team learns how to maintain the progress made in Sort, Set in order, and Shine stages, in the "Standardize" stage. They describe the easiest way to get the job done in a safe and efficient manner, give people adequate time to do what needs to be done, and post cleaning guidelines.

Then they move on to "Sustain," or making it their habit to maintain good 5S practices. Periodic evaluations, feedback on action plan results, and employee "ownership" of results drive continuing progress.

# Audit Process: A Needed Change

Eric Larson, project manager and 5S facilitator, noted that Elgin Sweeper found a formal audit process was needed to sustain the improvements achieved during lean events such as 5S, kaizen, and pull systems projects. This process was developed with input from employees in various functional areas and launched in the second half of 2003.

Sixteen volunteer auditors from the shop and office each review two areas per week. After checking a database to identify the areas they'll evaluate, auditors work against standard forms (5S audit, pull card, and two-bin forms that can be quickly printed out). A sample 5S audit form is shown in Figure 3.

The auditors rate a particular work center for 5S and pull systems and give copies of their audit to the supervisors who share them with work center associates. Copies are centrally located; they can be accessed by any associate. Supervisors maintain a master scorecard for all work centers in their department. Work centers scoring below 75 percent of acceptable performance will require action such as another 5S blitz event, pull systems rework, etc.

# Lean in the Office Environment

After a couple of years implementing pull systems and implementing layout changes using the 5S blitz process, the Lean Steering Committee determined that it was time to leverage lean concepts in the office environment. The manufacturing engineering office space was targeted for the first office 5S blitz. Several dumpsters were filled with discards during the two-day event. Participants improved the common printer/library area. Several desks were repositioned for easier information sharing. The 5S blitz process was later used in the accounting department; it was scheduled before an accounting kaizen blitz to introduce lean to this part of the organization. Engineering area "before" and "after" photos are shown in Figure 4. All office areas held 5S blitzes during 2003. Many office functions launched their own lean projects.

# Lessons Learned

Plant Manager Roger Himrod reported many "lessons learned" from Elgin Sweeper's lean cultural transformation. He noted:

5S Office Audit Form

| No | Description | Score | Comments |
|---|---|---|---|
| | **Sort & Set In Order: get rid of what isn't needed and organize.** | | |
| 1 | Equipment, files, supplies are accessible and ready to use. | | |
| 2 | Items put away when not in use. | | |
| 3 | Files, Folders and reference materials are neat, labeled and relevant to current work. | | |
| 4 | Files/folders and general office supplies are in use if away from the normal storage locations. | | |
| 5 | File Cabinets/organizers, Reference Materials, and in/out boxes are organized and labeled. | | |
| | **Shine** *plus Safety* | | |
| 6 | Equipment, floors and workplace are clean and free of debris. | | |
| 7 | Aisles and walkways are free of material. | | |
| 8 | Garbage and other waste materials are removed in a timely fashion. | | |
| 9 | Fire extinguishers and other safety equipment are clearly labeled, unobstructed and fully functional | | |
| 10 | Appropriate safety requirements, evacuation and emergency procedures etc. are clearly posted and adhered to. | | |
| | **Standardized:** *consistency of work processes and practices.* | | |
| 11 | Work instructions, computer programs (screens) are easy to understand. | | |
| 12 | Office equipment,file cabinets, etc are properly labeled. | | |
| 13 | Work areas utilize visual instructions where practical. | | |
| 14 | Preventive maintenance sheets are posted. | | |
| 15 | Standard work guidelines and procedures are posted | | |
| | **Sustain:** *following the set procedures over time* | | |
| 16 | People understand and follow the standards set for the area. | | |
| 17 | Team members do their jobs in a consistent manner. | | |
| 18 | Standards are considered targets for improvement with systems to promote on-going improvement at work site. | | |
| 19 | Visible performance feedback tools are up-to-date and used in the work area. | | |
| 20 | Bulletin boards are arranged neatly and with no out-of-date information or announcements. | | |
| | **Totals** | | |

Scoring: 0 = NA, 1 = Poor, 2 = Fair, 3 = Good, 4 = Excellent, 5 = World class        5s office Audit Form  before and after scores.xls    2/25/2004

## Figure 3.

- Support is needed from all management
- Engage supervisors (don't launch projects in a vacuum)
- Balance cross-functional resources (manufacturing engineering, production, materials, etc.)
- Dedicated resources such as "ME techs"

**Figure 4.** "Before 5S" and the amazing "after 5S" views in engineering.

- Additional training and understanding are needed
- "Sustain" is the most difficult challenge
- Take risks for better results.

## LES Results

| | |
|---|---|
| Capacity | Improved 37 percent |
| Inventory turns | Increased 52 percent |
| OSHA Injury Index | 41 percent improvement |
| Sales/employee | Increased 28 percent |
| ROS (return on sales) | Improved 15 percent |
| Space savings | 25 percent |

"A huge challenge everyone discovered after our initial 5S events was how difficult it is to sustain improvements several months after the events are held," said Himrod. He noted that the audit step in the 5S event process helped to prevent slippage after related events conclude.

"Lean is here to stay in our organization. "It's not the 'flavor of the month,'" said Himrod. "It's about continuous change." He added that 5S blitz events and related improvements affect every area of the operation. The 5S blitz event was used to impart lean concepts and lean thinking to employees. A total of 90+ employees (plant and office) have received lean training and held 5S events. This approach has contributed to overall attitude changes about lean ideas and accelerated lean activities enterprise-wide.

### Editor's notes

*Additional presenters and tour leaders in the recent AME event at Elgin Sweeper included: Jay Chandran, materials manager; Jim Feltes, business manager; Brad Splinter, business manager; Jeanne Hem, former lean coordinator; Dave Eakins, project manager; Eric Larson, project manager; and Al Collins, ME tech/5S coordinator. The assistance of Jay Chandran and Dave Eakins in the development of this article is appreciated. The author, a dedicated "pileontologist" (dedicated to the creation, movement, sorting, and occasional disposition of accumulated materials) for some years, confesses that a tiny bit of guilt about the condition of her office emerged, after viewing the "before" and "after" photos in Elgin Sweeper's engineering department (there were a few similarities in the "before" version); that regret has passed, replaced by a renewed effort to keep 5S in mind from time to time and the pleasant surprise that beneath various paperwork piles formerly occupying her work area there is a wood table surface; to be continued…*

*Lea A.P. Tonkin,* **Target** *editor, lives in Woodstock, IL.*

## Questions

How do you select 5S projects? For business impact? To leverage cultural change?

Do you have a sponsor and a facilitator for each 5S blitz?

Does each blitz team have a charter?

Is 5S training provided close to the time of the actual event?

Are your 5S events followed by audits to sustain improvement?

# Section III

# Lean in Healthcare

# 8

# Metamorphosis: Healthcare's Ongoing Transformation

Healing and cultural change have begun.

*Lea A.P. Tonkin*

## In Brief

Are you and your employees treated as first-class customers by your healthcare providers, at a reasonable cost? Patient safety problems, extended wait times, and steeply rising costs are more typical scenarios for many healthcare consumers. This article offers accounts of collaborative improvement initiatives. The remedy for healthcare's ills is well-known to manufacturing types who set their sights on world-class performance: a consistent, organization-wide focus on quality, complemented by teamwork, standardized performance criteria, information transparency, and perhaps most challenging of all, cultural change.

Imagine that you and your employees could be treated as first-class customers by your healthcare providers —your time valued, your problems heard, and your needs attended to in an effective and safe manner, with no extended wait times, and that these services need not cost more than previous care. And if your hospital or doctor or other providers made an error such as giving you the wrong medication, would you ex-pect to receive an honest report about the incident and to learn what improvements are underway to eliminate the root cause of the mistake? For many of us, this scenario is just a dream.[1,2] Yet encouraging changes are underway. Following are accounts of healthcare improvement initiatives—a number patterned after lean or continuous improvement activities that manufacturing folks have been implementing over the years.

Just as manufacturing people learned long ago, computerizing the whole healthcare shebang won't cut it.[3,4] A consistent, organization-wide focus on quality, complemented by teamwork, standardized performance criteria, information transparency, and perhaps most challenging of all, cultural change are critical to performance improvement. To learn how you can become part of this metamorphosis, read on.

## ThedaCare's Lean Efforts

When Dr. John Toussaint, president and CEO of ThedaCare™ addressed the 2004 AME annual conference, he shared how a health-care delivery system uses lean approaches to better its quality and cost performance. ThedaCare, an Appleton, WI-community health system, encompasses three hospitals, as well as physicians, behavioral health, at-home care, and senior services, and a retirement living community, assisted living, and skilled nursing facilities. Its joint ventures include a community clinic, the Appleton Heart Institute, an ambulance service, and ThedaCare Physicians' Shawano Family Medicine. Dr. Toussaint said the two key goals for ThedaCare's overall lean efforts are, "1) We must lower our costs, so that we can lower the price you pay for our services, and 2) we simultaneously must improve the quality of what we do to world-class levels (95th percentile)."

Thanks to their lean focus launched in 2002 and other improvement efforts, initial results are encouraging:
- Saved $154,000 in operating room procurement processes
- Improved cash flow by $8.1 million
- Reduced staff (32 staff positions) resulting in no service reduction or layoffs (turnover is about ten percent)
- Dramatically cut clinical documentation cycle time (50 percent)
- Telephone triage times decreased from 89 seconds to 28 seconds (patients connected to a nurse or appropriate personnel), while triage abandonment (people hanging up) dropped from 11.6 percent to 0.6 percent
- Improved productivity related to new staff hiring, for a $235,000 savings in staff time.

## Treating Patients as Customers

These selected examples may have dollar signs attached, but the emphasis on patients—treating them as customers—is clear. "We look at what we can deliver to the customer, at the value proposition," Dr.

## IHI's 100k Lives Campaign

The Institute for Healthcare Improvement (IHI), joining with other health-care organizations, launched a "100k Lives Campaign," aiming to enlist participation by thousands of hospitals across the United States. The campaign to make healthcare more safe and effective, achieving the best possible outcomes for all patients, is among various IHI healthcare improvement initiatives.

Contending that widely-implemented healthcare improvements can prevent 100,000 avoidable deaths a year, the IHI started with six recommended interventions:

- Deploy rapid response teams
- Deliver reliable, evidence-based care for acute myocardial infarction
- Prevent adverse drug effects (ADEs)
- Prevent central line (large IVs inserted into the neck or chest) infections
- Prevent surgical site infections
- Prevent ventilator-associated pneumonia.

"The names of patients whose lives we can save can never be known," said Don M. Berwick, M.D., M.P.P., IHI's president and CEO and an ardent champion of healthcare improvement. He added that more grandfathers will attend graduations and weddings they would have missed, grandchildren will know their grandparents they might not have known, books will be read, and gardens will be tended that, without this improvement work, would never have happened.

IHI has gathered statistics indicating that as many as 98,000 people die in U.S. hospitals each year related to medical injuries; an estimated two million patients get hospital-acquired infections every year; and that the United States spends the highest amount for healthcare among (advanced) industrialized nations while performing more poorly than most countries on healthcare quality measures.

Toussaint said. "For example, I recently sat in with a team at one of our clinics, while they were working to reduce triage abandonment rates. They previously had patient reps answering all calls. The reps had a lot of paperwork steps to get data for the patient. The team redesigned the system so reps schedule patients for appointments and blood tests, while other requests requiring nursing feedback go into a nursing triage system. That dramatically reduced waiting time and the patients talk to a nurse if that is needed.

"In our system, you can go online and see when the next appointment is needed. We have an open access system. Not much is scheduled, because we work on supply and demand," he continued. "You can plug in that you want a 6 p.m. appointment if that is open, on the same day.

"It isn't just about lowering costs," Dr. Toussaint added. "It's about improving service and morale. The typical healthcare administrator doesn't have a clue about connecting cost and quality. We've got to figure this out. American industry has been at this lean approach for a long time now. The Toyota Production System (TPS) is what our industry needs, and that doesn't make everyone in our industry happy."

Calling on manufacturing practitioners to share their knowledge about lean improvements with the healthcare industry, Dr. Toussaint noted that people from Wisconsin snow blower manufacturer Ariens had shared their lean "lessons learned" with ThedaCare personnel. "They worked with us to analyze our value streams, and we had visits back and forth," he recalled. "Industry leaders can get involved, pushing healthcare leaders to get involved in lean, because it works—affecting productivity, defect rates, and morale."

A "big believer" in standard performance criteria and public reporting, Dr. Toussaint said ThedaCare has been reporting on mortality rates for years. He is chairman of the Wisconsin Collaborative for Healthcare Quality (www.wchq.org) which advocates such disclosure. "There is a need for standard benchmarks or common definitions," he added. "The centers for Medicare and Medicaid are beginning to develop measures." ThedaCare also participates in the Institute of Healthcare Improvement (IHI) organization's 100k Lives Campaign goal of saving 100,000 lives in 2005 and every year thereafter through proven interventions (see the box, "IHI's 100k Lives Campaign").

"This isn't a project," Dr. Toussaint emphasized. "If it's only a project, you'll never get long-term benefits. What we need is cultural transformation."

ThedaCare's current improvement activities target three areas. First is quality. They are working to improve their smoking cessation counseling for people who have had heart attacks and ensure that discharged heart failure patients receive the most appropriate medications.

Second, they're also aiming to reduce overall expenses $10 million annually. "We're about $3 million towards that goal," said Dr. Toussaint. ThedaCare monthly spends about $64,000 to run an average 20 improvement events, while generating an average of approximately $200,000 a month in estimated annualized savings from these events.

The people side of improvement is the "third leg of the stool." Their goal is to be on Fortune's top employer list. "If you can't afford to make improvements, then I question why you are in the business," said the doctor. "It's all about the best care and information, at the lowest cost."

## Pulling Together in Iowa

The quest for healthcare improvement through collaborative efforts is gaining momentum in many areas and organizations. "In a November, 2002 Des Moines conference, 'A New Vision for Health Care—Forging Partnerships for Business, Consumers, and Health Care Providers,' lean was one of the key ideas of this new vision," recalled Paul Pietzsch, president of Health Policy Corporation of Iowa (HPCI). The conference was sponsored by numerous organizations including HPCI and the Iowa Association of Business and Industry, the Iowa Hospital Association (IHA), the Iowa Medical Association, the Iowa Nurses Association, the Iowa Federation of Labor AFL/CIO, and the Iowa Department of Public Health. It drew approximately 250 attendees.

The Iowa Business Council helped organize a conference session on lean enterprise. An Iowa manufacturer, HON industries (now HNI Corporation), described lean operations and related improvements. "We also had a panel discussion on lean enterprise and healthcare. We are fortunate to have Iowa manufacturers step up and be willing to assist in engaging lean in the healthcare sector," said Pietzsch. "The concept of applying lean to healthcare was new to some attendees. Besides, they were already working on improvement." But there was interest in exploring lean healthcare further.

Next, the Iowa Business Council, HPCI, and others pulled together a task force of healthcare, industry, and others to pursue the lean enterprise–healthcare connection. "In July, 2003 Maytag sponsored a value stream mapping (VSM) program at their corporate headquarters in Newton, IA," said Pietzsch. "It had three components: healthcare delivery or patient care services, administration, and customer focus. A detailed map of the current state for billing, claims, and payment processes was developed. At this point, we decided to focus on several identified 'areas of opportunity' (heartburns) and administrative costs—that's where a third of healthcare dollars go," he said of the collaborative task force efforts.

In early 2004, the Iowa Coalition for Innovation and Growth, sponsored by the Iowa Business Council and the Iowa Chamber of

Commerce, and HPCI formed a healthcare Hot Team of business leaders, healthcare providers, the IHA, the insurance industry, and others. Among corporations represented on the Hot Team have been senior executives from Pella Corporation, HNI Corporation, Vermeer, and Rockwell Collins.

The Hot Team decided to do kaizen (improvement) events during the summer of 2004 at three hospitals in Iowa—the University of Iowa Hospitals and Clinics in Iowa City, Unity Health System in Muscatine, and St. Luke's in Cedar Rapids. Working with the consulting firm TBM (they volunteered) and volunteers from industry as well as the IHA, the Hot Team looked for ways to introduce lean to the patient care side of healthcare through kaizen event pilots or demonstrations. Results from these three pilots included: 1) Removed a two-week CT (computerized tomography) scan process backlog, processing four more patients a day; 2) implemented a process to increase the percentage of time a patient is transported within a 20-minute window from 90 percent to 98 percent; and 3) decreased patient leadtime for acute care processing by 25 percent. The Hot Team is planning a second round of kaizen events. HPCI is continuing to work with healthcare organizations, employers, lean practitioners/experts, and others to create better linkages and common metrics between healthcare providers and the external customer.

## University of Iowa Hospitals and Clinics: Patients Wait Less, Higher Productivity

Trimming wasted, non-value-added (NVA) steps during one of the Hot Team's 2004 pilots helped personnel at the University of Iowa Hospitals and Clinics (UIHC) in Iowa City get patients in more promptly for their CT scans, for example. "Fortunately, executives from Pella and Maytag were with us during a kaizen event, for an entire week," said Ann Madden Rice, chief operating officer. "While we had invested in equipment that worked well, we had a lot of wait time between scans. During the kaizen event, we eliminated the waiting time between when a patient goes to the registration clerk and when the patient is given a contrast fluid to drink." They also placed a small refrigerator near the registration desk for the fluid, and gave the registration clerk a script so that the patient received standardized information. Once the patient drank the contrast fluid, a nurse was called to start an IV (generally needed when a patient takes the contrast fluid), eliminating another waiting period. They also found that medical assistants (instead of radiology technicians doing this task) could position patients with the equipment and help in multiple rooms, giving radiologists more time to complete the scan. "By following and mapping footsteps of who moved where, we found that the staff previously made many extra steps," said Rice. "We were able to increase the number of scans a day by about 20 percent. Patients are always happy when they have to spend less time waiting for a test, and the staff felt that their time was used more productively."

"Encouraged by these initial results, University of Iowa Hospitals and Clinics personnel have more kaizen projects such as catheterization labs and out-patient clinics in mind," Rice said. More lean training through the Iowa Business Council and Rockwell Collins personnel were on the agenda early this year. Rice believes that improvement activities, using a variety of tools, not only eliminate waste but also contribute to reduction in potential errors.

## Hot Team's Revving Up More Collaboration

"One of the things that developed out of these initial kaizen events in Iowa was that all three hospitals got excited about rapid process improvement utilizing the kaizen methodology. By sharing their finds with others in the healthcare field, they generated more interest from other Iowa healthcare providers. To date, at least three additional hospitals have asked for industry to come alongside and jumpstart their improvement efforts," said Vince Newendorp, chairman of the Iowa healthcare Hot Team and vice president of administration for Pella, IA-based Vermeer Manufacturing Company.

"One of the many things we've learned in industry is that there's a need to develop a pull system based on customer need," said Newendorp. "By demonstrating that the lean enterprise tools are applicable in healthcare, genuine interest in the process has begun and industry is being asked to participate alongside additional healthcare providers. In addition to our involvement promoting kaizen events, our lean health-promoting kaizen events, our lean healthcare Hot Team has developed four supporting projects in 2005. One of these projects is a resource kit to be made available to the healthcare providers in Iowa, explaining lean enterprise methodology, an understanding of the tools that are available to them, offering real life testimonials of what lean has done in Iowa hospital settings, and identifying industry experts where lean has become a culture, not just a 'flavor of the month' in making significant improvement in quality, cost, delivery, and safety through waste elimination and process improvements. Another one of our projects includes inviting healthcare professionals to participate in future industry and healthcare kaizen events in Iowa—to be part of our improvement events—to get exposure to what lean is all about. We are also developing an understanding of what others are doing in the area of lean in healthcare outside of Iowa and what we could apply to the work we are doing here."

## Companies Teaming Up with Healthcare Providers

These healthcare improvement projects also blend well with the Iowa Coalition for Innovation and Growth's business boosting work, aimed at making the state more attractive to business, according to Dean Bliss, senior lean electronics consultant for Rockwell Collins, Cedar Rapids, IA. The coalition is a function of the Iowa Business Council (a board of CEOs of the 25 largest employers in Iowa).

"Healthcare costs are growing faster than any other element of cost," Bliss said. "What we've done in Iowa can be done through other organizations around the country. At the same time, the quality of patient care and patient safety cannot be compromised."

## Insurance Provider: A Need to Build Trust

One of the challenges confronting healthcare improvement practitioners is the belief that lean means skimpy services. Or that computerizing and automating processes will solve problems. "We need instead to find the root causes of problems or errors and then to eliminate them," said Dale Andringa, M.D., a member of the Iowa healthcare Hot Team and vice president of health management/chief medical officer for Wellmark Blue Cross and Blue Shield in Iowa. Dr. Andringa has been a physician for 28 years, and before joining Wellmark, he worked in private practice, the insurance industry, and corporate healthcare.

"There was little communication between providers of healthcare and employers in the past," he said. "While there are differences, we are finding more similarities. Clearly industry has been on a best practice path longer. We need to collaborate and exchange information."

> ## The Leapfrog Group
>
> Leapfrog Group members believe that, together, they can drive "great leaps" in patient safety and healthcare quality. These healthcare purchasers advocate using standard criteria for selection of hospitals, physicians, and other healthcare providers. Safe practices to promote patient safety recommended by the organization include:
>
> 1. Computer physician order entry (CPOE)
> 2. Evidence-based hospital referral (EHR)
> 3. ICU physician staffing (IPS)
> 4. National Quality Forum (NQF) safe practices.
>
> The first three criteria are recommended as the basis for healthcare provider performance comparisons as well as hospital recognition and reward. Research conducted by John D. Birkmeyer, M.D. of Dartmouth Medical School indicated that as many as 58,300 lives could be saved and 522,000 medication errors could be avoided annually from these three practices if they were used in all non-rural U.S. hospitals. The group noted that their recommendation does not imply a lack of other methods for assuring or improving patient safety (www.leapfroggroup.org).

He noted that many healthcare providers traditionally focused more on increasing revenue than on reducing costs.

While he strongly supports the Leapfrog Group (see the box, "The Leapfrog Group") efforts to broadly improve healthcare, Dr. Andringa perceives great value in "narrow, deep" improvement activities. "There has to be a commitment to bring all of the parties together in a non-threatening way," he said. "You need dialog to build trust, to create understanding that it's not about eliminating services." Shorter waiting times and improved accuracy in medication records, for example, find cheerleaders among the healthcare provider community as well as patients.

The insurance industry also needs to work on process improvements, said Dr. Andringa. "We at Wellmark have as a core value that we will be the easiest plan to do business with—responding quickly and when needed, with the right response," he said. An example is the company's medical review process. They are looking for root causes of errors when claims are filed, and then educating providers about how to file correctly to eliminate payment delays. "An example of eliminating NVA activities is that we have found mailing questions about incorrectly-filed claims leads to longer processing time, the doctor said. "Sometimes a quick phone call eliminates many of the questions as well as the old batch and queue system."

Dr. Andringa offered several suggestions for collaborative healthcare improvement champions: 1) build trust and relationships for mutual advantage; 2) people who can commit time over an extended period are needed from hospital, physician, industry, and other groups (if initial participation is meager and results require patience, that is not unexpected); 3) view these efforts as a journey rather than as a passing fad. During the past three years, Six Sigma efforts at Wellmark netted $41.4 million in cost savings. "I believe that with Six Sigma and rapid process improvement, this will increase exponentially," Dr. Andringa said.

## Virginia Mason Medical Center: Seeking Zero Defects Through the Application of the Toyota Production System

A few months following a chance meeting on an airplane between J. Michael Rona, the president of Virginia Mason Medical Center (VMMC) and John Black of Shingijutsu, USA (a former Boeing executive) in the fall of 2000, senior leadership at VMMC became convinced that there was a compelling connection between the future of healthcare delivery and the Toyota Production System (TPS, or lean) concepts. Leadership's commitment and understanding of how these principles could make healthcare safer and less expensive for the consumer grew after a series of training sessions and visits with Wiremold, Boeing, and Genie executives—all of whom had transformed their organizations by adopting TPS principles. Within months of first hearing about "lean," Dr. Gary Kaplan, chairman and CEO of VMMC and Mike Rona insisted that the most senior leaders at VMMC experience Toyota first hand. "The trip to Japan, which included visits to Toyota and a gemba kaizen event at Hitachi, revealed the tremendous level of commitment required for an organization to implement lean the way it should be—organization-wide," said Christina Saint Martin, administrative director of governance and administration. "Lean is not a quick fix; it takes decades to fully realize the tremendous opportunities kaizen has to offer," she said. "We came back with a commitment that this was the way we would go about our work—the way, from now on, that our processes would be improved."

Executives and administrators were trained intensively for six to eight months. Following a rigorous external assessment of the trainees, certification was awarded to those who passed the criteria and could competently run a Rapid Process Improvement Workshop (RPIW). RPIWs are weeklong, intensive workshops where the people who do the work improve their process and test the results. "We started with about 20 RPIWs the first year," said Saint Martin. Doctors, nurses, and others on a team (usually five to eight members/stakeholders) test and make changes during the week, then fully implement the changes the following week. "In 2004, we had about 220 RPIWs. We currently have 65 certified leaders; each one is required to run three workshops per year to maintain certification. Certification is a requirement for all executives and administrative directors. We've worked diligently on leadtime reduction (less patient waiting time), eliminating defects, processing time, staff walking distance, patient walking distance, inventory, productivity, and setup reduction. We have actually eliminated large waiting rooms in some areas where patients used to have several waiting periods," said Saint Martin. "Current RPIW targets are much more specific than in initial events, bringing even better results in primary care, the hospital, and our administrative services. We share our results at report-out every Friday and staff members can also access database information on the RPIWs to share improvements across the organization and avoid 'reinventing the wheel.'

"It's all based on the value stream map (VSM), eliminating waste and providing only value to our customers. For example, eliminating NVA activities for nurses gives them more time to spend with patients," continued Saint Martin. "Managers are required to attend VSM, standard operations, 5S and mistake-proofing classes and complete assignments for each course. We see training as a key component in our success and we also have training for our 4,500 non-management staff.

"We're not going to solve world hunger in one workshop—there's a need to be aware of 'scope creep,'" Saint Martin said. "You need to be specific. For example, reducing leadtime for the clinical laboratory collection list. One RPIW team created standard work, went from batch processing to one-piece flow, and designed a Just-In-Time (JIT) dispatch system. They reduced staff walking time 42 percent, decreased leadtime 50 percent, eliminated more than half the work in progress (WIP) bottlenecks, and improved productivity by 20 percent."

Saint Martin added that RPIWs help to streamline administrative processes such as capital budgeting. The old batch process used to leave people in the dark about their request for as much as 16-18 months. An RPIW team spent a week improving the process and developing standard processes and filters for making requests, she said. Requests must include information about what the applicant wants and why (ask why five times to get to the reason—patient safety, cost reduction, etc.). The new single-piece flow brings a response within ten days. Many requests are handled quickly by an administrative director who can approve items $10,000 and below, or by managers who can approve requests at $2,500 and below.

## Patient Safety: 5S, Andon Lights, "Stopping the Line"

Patient safety is the most important focus at VMMC. Staff members used exercises to think "out of the box" for ways to eliminate mislabeling patient records, IVs, etc. They reference the Institute of Medicine's (IOM) related counsel. One solution is the "It Takes Two" approach—meaning that it takes two identifiers such as birth date or Social Security Number to identify a patient (in case a patient is incoherent or a patient's armband is incorrect, for example). 5S efforts, over time, ensure that equipment, manuals, charts, furniture, files, etc. are where they are supposed to be. Andon lights on some equipment remind staff to test daily when needed.

Another organization-wide patient safety initiative is the Patient Safety Alert System (PSAS). After studying the Toyota system which enables workers on the production line to "pull the cord" if errors occur during production (stopping the line until the error is eliminated), they developed the PSAS for all staff so that unsafe processes or individuals practicing in an unsafe manner can be "taken off the line" when there is a problem such as medication safety (for example, wrong blood type about to be administered to a patient). When such an alert occurs, the area manager and vice president and/or clinical chief go to the area, the Patient Safety Department is notified, and they do root cause analysis to resolve the issue within 24 hours.

VMMC's work over the past three years created a revolutionary change in its culture of medicine and healthcare management. Their personnel learned that they could progress toward the goal of becoming a quality leader in healthcare by following Toyota management principles: Put the customer first; be relentless about quality and zero defects; create an absolutely safe environment; create a work environment in which workers can excel; and eliminate waste in all processes.

They also learned that the rigorous pursuit of quality would be profitable because of the elimination of waste and dramatic productivity improvements.

## Cancer Treatment Centers of America: Lean Thinking Reduces Errors

Properly applied, lean thinking principles enhanced patient safety by reducing errors, added Carol Lepper, RN, MBA, director of Lean Operations for Cancer Treatment Centers of America at Midwestern Regional Medical Center, Zion, IL.[5] For example, patient safety is the most important factor of pharmaceutical services, she said. They set a goal to increase patient safety by improving turn-around-time (TAT) 20 percent for the preparation, dispensing, and delivery process for chemotherapy medication orders. A lean team composed of pharmacy staff used tools such as VSM, 5S visual workplace, standard work instructions (SWIs), work flow redesign, and inventory management in the pharmacy area. They documented and eliminated waste in areas such as information flow (duplications, other wastes), unnecessary walking, scheduling, load balance issues, queue time, and supply disruptions.

After developing a chemotherapy safety log, SWIs, a just-in-time inventory management system for IV supplies, and visual workplace changes (such as visuals for work flow and standard locations for supplies), they recorded dramatic improvements. Process steps decreased 50 percent; walk distance (feet per day) dropped 43 percent; average TAT for chemotherapy improved 37 percent. Self-reported chemotherapy errors also decreased. "Lean thinking is a new way of thinking," Lepper said. "We learned to triage our orders by complexity, thus reducing overall TAT without compromising patient safety."

## Partnership, Disclosing Errors Without Blame, and Other Critical Success Factors

An emphasis on process improvement encompassing seven Critical Success Factors (CSFs) for reducing hospital errors was suggested by Dr. Kathleen L. McFadden of Northern Illinois University (NIU),

Elizabeth R. Towell of Carroll College, and Gregory N. Stock, NIU.[6] The CSFs included 1) partnership of all stakeholders—gathering information from a variety of perspectives; 2) reporting errors without blame—replacing the fear of retribution for reporting healthcare errors; 3) open-ended focus groups; 4) cultural shift—where knowledge is shared and information flows freely in an open environment; 5) education and training programs; 6) statistical analysis of error data; and 7) system redesign—it may encompass reduction of scope (possibly using simple procedures to replace one that is more complex), the addition of process steps/constraints/new technology, or other changes that make it difficult or impossible to make certain errors.

Although there are significant differences between aviation and healthcare, McFadden and Towell noted that there are similarities with implications for error management.[7] For example, aviation near misses as well as failures are reported and analyzed, then root causes of error are determined so they can be eliminated. A more recent report by McFadden and colleagues G. Stock and C. Gowen, based on a survey sample of 133 hospitals, indicated that the more importance a hospital places on the qualitative seven CSFs, the more likely it is to implement them.[8] Their research also showed that hospital managers need to remove barriers that may limit needed cultural changes or other improvements. "What's important is that hospitals implement process changes as a 'package' together," said McFadden.

## "No One Goes to Work Intending to Hurt Anybody"

Lean is not about eliminating the compassionate, personal approach or eliminating professional judgment in healthcare. It is finding ways to make people's jobs better and easier so they can eliminate errors and waste, spending more time with patients and working on healthcare quality improvements, according to Cindy Jimmerson, principal of Lean Healthcare West consulting firm.[9] Much of her healthcare improvement work stems from earlier research funded by the National Science Foundation.

Jimmerson advocates using TPS principles to reduce errors and waste, while improving workplace morale. In one hospital intensive care unit improvement event example, a team looked for ways to eliminate medication errors related to the wrong IV drip rate; seven such errors had been reported in a three-month period. Work improvements made by the team included standardizing the way to calculate medication drip rates and report activity, and calibrating all IV monitoring machines the same. The result was no medication errors related to the wrong rate in the subsequent three months and a feeling of confidence by the staff that all medications were being delivered safely.

Jimmerson shared lessons learned from healthcare improvement activities at various hospitals: Senior leadership buy-in and participation are critical to the success of these efforts; be thoughtful about aims/goals; have courage to make way for new processes and ideas, despite sometimes-strong resistance; communicate effectively; invest in support for long-term cultural change.

"We need to make a case for change," Jimmerson said. "No one goes to work intending to hurt anybody. But healthcare systems are complex. We need to get people to stop and look at their work differently, and we need people in manufacturing and others to share how they've implemented lean and how it can be applied in healthcare."

## The Need for Greater Transparency

Is there a means to "spread the gospel" of healthcare improvement more widely? Among the organizations working toward improving healthcare quality and efficiency is the Consumer–Purchaser Disclosure Project. It is a coalition of purchaser, consumer, and labor organizations that have joined forces to improve the availability of information about the performance of hospitals, physicians, and other providers. "The unique aspect of the Disclosure Project is that we've united the 'buy side' of the market and are collaborating to ensure that many of the national quality efforts underway in the marketplace reflect the needs of purchasers and consumers," said Katherine Browne, managing director of the Consumer–Purchaser Disclosure Project.

Francois de Brantes, General Electric's program leader for healthcare initiatives in corporate Health Care, said the first goal of the Consumer–Purchaser Disclosure Project is to create greater transparency. "There is very little information you can rely on for finding better-performing hospitals and physicians," he said. "We need better information on our suppliers to act in a rational way. There is no reason to treat healthcare differently from the way you would treat any other supply chain. The major source of information corporations rely on is cost, which is insufficient. We have found that higher quality can be associated with lower cost, but not always, so you need more reliable information in the market." The

Disclosure Project has issued a set of guidelines that all health plans can apply to increase the amount of information on physicians and hospitals in a uniform manner.

de Brantes noted that the American Medical Association has worked with the National Quality Forum, the National Committee for Quality Assurance, and other organizations to develop clarity in performance measures. If providers are asked to meet inconsistent standards, the result would be more costly and disruptive. "We don't want to make this punitive. But providers and consumers are not getting the right types of signals," said de Brantes. "We need consistency across

## Resources

- ASQ: See the organization's website (www.asq.org); among recent newsroom headings was, "Children's Hospital Using Six Sigma to Improve Imaging Technology;" ASQ Quality Press offers a Healthcare Library of published materials.
- Baldrige Award (Malcolm Baldrige National Quality Award); at the website www.nist.gov. search for the awards, then among the recipients you can check healthcare recipients, then see quality and improvement results, and related areas.
- Bridges to Excellence: "Rewarding quality across the healthcare system" is the objective of this organization. They seek to create programs that will align everyone's incentives around higher quality: reengineering care processes to reduce mistakes, reducing defects to decrease waste and inefficiencies in the healthcare system, and raising accountability as well as encouraging quality improvements by releasing comparative provider performance data to consumers (website www.bridgestoexcellence.org).
- Consumer–Purchaser Disclosure Project: employer, consumer, and labor organizations working together to ensure that Americans have access to publicly-reported healthcare performance information; at their website www.healthcaredisclosure.org, more information is available about their vision that Americans could select physicians, hospitals, and treatments based on nationally-standardized measures (clinical quality, consumer experience, equity, and efficiency) and related strategies.
- HealthGrades: This healthcare quality ratings and services company studies patient safety incidents and other healthcare issues, recognizes hospitals for distinguished patient safety performance, offers healthcare provider ratings/profiles, and has "how to choose" information on methodologies (www.healthgrades.com).

the country to say that it doesn't matter if you are in Peoria or Columbus—you should be able to know if a doctor delivers quality in diabetes care, for example."

Having performance information publicly reported and changing the way providers are reimbursed is critical so that high quality and efficient care are rewarded. "Let's install normal market discipline, directing incentives to doctors and hospitals for those who do well, and incentives for consumers to consume in the right places—such as co-pays based on the value created by the doctor or the hospital," de Brantes said.

- Institute for Healthcare Improvement (IHI) organization; information on its 100k Lives Campaign and other activities is on the website www.ihi.org.
- Leapfrog Group (The): Their website www.leapfroggroup.org offers information about initiatives to improve patient safety and healthcare quality; the organization encourages the use of standard criteria for selecting hospitals and other healthcare providers. Information on additional healthcare performance improvement initiatives is provided—for example, National Quality Forum (NQF) Safe Practices, plus links to groups such as Employer Health Care Alliance Cooperative (www.alliancehealthcoop.com), The National Business Coalition on Health (www.nbch.org), The Joint commission Accreditation of Health Care Organizations (www.jcaho.org), The American Hospital Association (www.aha.org), and others.
- National Patient Safety Foundation®: This national organization offers a broad range of education and awareness programs and resources as well as links to patient safety websites (see their website www.npsf.org). It aims to improve patient safety in the delivery of healthcare by identifying and creating a core body of knowledge, identifying pathways to apply this knowledge, develop and enhance the culture of receptivity to patient safety, and raise public awareness about patient safety.
- National Quality Forum (NQF); the private, not-for-profit membership organization seeks endorsement of consensus-based national standards for measurement and public reporting of healthcare performance data offering information about whether care is safe, timely, beneficial, patient-centered, equitable, and efficient. Among reports are national priorities for quality measurement and reporting, national voluntary consensus standards for nursing-sensitive care, etc. (www.qualityforum.org).

GE supports the efforts of the Leapfrog Group (using standard criteria for selecting hospitals—see the related accompanying box) and Bridges to Excellence (see below) on the physician side. "We've created incentives for physicians to improve their performance," de Brantes said. "The message is that if you meet performance measures and deliver good care, we will give you more money."

The Bridges to Excellence coalition is an organization of large employers, health plans, the National Committee for Quality Assurance, and other groups that supports physician pay-for-performance efforts. The not-for-profit group encourages significant improvements in healthcare quality by recognizing and rewarding healthcare providers demonstrating delivery of safe, timely, effective, efficient, and patient-centered care. The National Business Coalition on Health (NBCH), an organization of employer-based coalitions, selected four Bridges to Excellence demonstration sites. They paid out $800,000 to 35 medical groups in the Boston area to reward systems implementation and leveraging information technology to track and educate patients, maintain medical records, prescribe medicines, and ensure appropriate follow-up.

## Peg Healthcare Buys to Quality

Quality-based purchasing of healthcare services is drawing greater attention and converts. The Employer Health Care Alliance Cooperative (The Alliance) hosted a related conference in Madison, WI last year to bring together executives from various companies implementing practices such as lean manufacturing and Six Sigma with healthcare providers, representatives from ASQ, and others.

"One of the many challenges in transforming healthcare is a deeply-rooted cultural norm that venerates professional autonomy," said Chris Queram, CEO of the Alliance. "Many healthcare professionals believe that you can't standardize protocols and treatments. However, there is growing consensus that standard protocols and procedures can reduce variation in care and improve performance in a large number of conditions and diagnoses."

Queram added, "We as purchasers need to do a better job of developing healthcare purchasing specifications. We can insist on more evidence of quality improvement activities. We can showcase and support early adopters, to learn from them what's worked and how we can replicate these efforts. As an example, we are in the early stages of reengineering our contracting activities so as to place a greater emphasis on improving healthcare quality. In the past, multi-year contracts were tied to cost of living or other measures. Now we are in the process of tying these agreements to quality improvements."[10]

*Editor's note: The assistance of Paul Pietzsch, HPCI; Cindy Jimmerson, Lean Healthcare West; and Ev Dale, Dale & Associates in the development of this article is appreciated.*

*Lea A. P. Tonkin, Woodstock, IL is the editor of* Target *Magazine.*

## Footnotes

1. Wachter, Robert M., M.D. and Kaveh G. Shojania, M.D., *Internal Bleeding: The Truth Behind America's Terrifying Epidemic of Medical Mistakes,* Rugged Land, LLC, New York City, NY, 2004, pp. 83-98.
2. "HealthGrades Quality Study: Patient Safety in American Hospitals, July 2004," released by HealthGrades, 2004; see the organization's website, www.health-grades.com; the report indicated that, despite widely-publicized information on preventable deaths cause by medical errors in U.S. hospitals, little evidence could show patient safety improvement during the past five years. The study referenced an earlier Institute of Medicine (IOM) report that an estimated 98,000 Americans are lost from preventable deaths related to medical errors every year (see, *To Err is Human: Building a Safer Health System,* edited by L.T. Kohn, J.M. Corrigan, and M.S. Donaldson, National Academy Press, Washington, 1999).
3. Gibson, Rosemary and Janardan Prasad Singh, *Wall of Silence: The Untold Story of the Medical Mistakes That Kill and Injure Millions of Americans:* Lifeline Press, Washington, D.C., 2003, pp. 176-179.
4. Deyo, Richard A., M.D., M.P.H., and Donald L. Patrick, Ph.D., M.S.P.H., *Hope or Hype: The Obsession with Medical Advances and the High Cost of False Promises,* AMA-COM, New York, NY, 2005, pp. 27-51.
5. Carol Lepper, RN, MBA, of Cancer Treatment Centers of America at Midwestern Regional Medical Center was a presenter at the 2004 AME annual conference.
6. McFadden, Kathleen L., Elizabeth R. Towell, and Gregory N. Stock, "Critical Success Factors for Controlling and Managing Hospital Errors," *Quality Management Journal,* Vol. 11, issue 1, pp. 61-74.
7. McFadden, K.L., and E.R. Towell, "Aviation Human Factors: A Framework for the New Millennium," *Journal of Air Transport Management,* 5, 1999, pp. 177-184.
8. McFadden, K.L., C.R. Gowen, and G.N. Stock, "Implementing an Error Management System for Improving Patient Safety," Proceeding of the 2004 Annual Meeting of Decision Sciences Institute, Boston, MA, November, 2004.
9. Cindy Jimmerson, Lean Healthcare West was a presenter at the 2004 AME annual conference.

10. An additional example of corporate initiatives to encourage higher performance in the healthcare field was the August 23, 2004 article, "Provider, Heal Thyself," by David Phelps, in the *Minneapolis Star Tribune,* citing General Motors' process improvement activities with insurer/provider Health Partners.

---

## Questions

Do your healthcare administrators understand the relationship between cost and quality?

Is your focus on adding value (providing quality service) to patients?

Is your healthcare organization working with industry to learn about process improvement?

Are you working with insurers to achieve improvements?

Does your organization believe that computerization will solve most problems?

Do your contracts with outside organizations focus on improving quality?

---

# "The Calling:" St. Vincent Hospice

*Robert W. Hall*

## In Brief

St. Vincent Hospice illustrates lessons relevant to the behavioral side of process excellence. Rather than by rigorous implementation of improvement techniques, quality performance comes from the intense dedication of staff and volunteers to their core mission. They cultivate work culture capabilities that would not ordinarily occur to a manufacturing company.

As far removed from manufacturing as anything can be, St. Vincent Hospice in Indianapolis is a study of excellence in working culture. A typical word of mouth recommendation is, "If you need a hospice, they're the best." Its medical procedures are well done, but not technically novel; its improvement techniques are not benchmarks.

But St. Vincent's has something worth studying, a working culture based on respect for all people. "Respect for People" is one of the twin "pillars" of the Toyota Way, right up there with "Continuous Improvement," and as everyone discovers, eliminating waste by engineering the techniques hits a limit without addressing how we have to change.[1] This "lesson" is how St. Vincent's working culture makes its performance "a cut above."

Much of the public has never heard of hospice care. If they have, their knowledge is usually foggy. Because hospice care differs in intent from curative care, it also befuddles many medical professionals. Clarifying misconceptions is a part of daily operations within St. Vincent, and explaining it over and over when people are emotional tries the patience. Compared with the St. Vincent staff, Job had attention deficit disorder.

A hospice is not a hospital. Hospitals are for acute care curative medicine. A hospice serves the terminally ill and their families in the last six months of life, after no further measures to restore health are expected to succeed. Most patients are past the prime of life, but not all. St. Vincent has a hospice for children too. They don't convert raw emotion into product; they convert raw emotion into something peaceful.

## Why Hospice Care is Growing

Retirement plans, including retiree health care expenses, have become a handicap to U.S. global competitiveness. Old companies whose retirees outnumber current employees are especially hard hit. GM's future liability to retirees now exceeds $60 billion, their heaviest financial burden. Comparably high retirement loads helped sink several old steel companies into bankruptcy, and end-of-life care is a big share of that expense.[2]

From 1900-2000, life expectancy in North America and other developed economies increased by about 30 years. Toward the end of our extended lives, many of us will acquire ailments that few of our forebears lived long enough to contract. Infections of various kinds took them before the onset of Alzheimer's or other senile infirmities that may not be the final cause of death. And during extended disability, our family caregivers are likely to be fully employed or geographically remote. Extended care facilities—nursing homes—have become big business (see Figure 1).

During the past century, medicine became ever more technological, expensive too. With an ever-bigger arsenal of techniques to try, physicians don't give up on a patient until they have exhausted their stock of miracles. Consequently, nearly 80 percent of deaths in the United States occur in hospitals or nursing homes, where dying is seen more as a clinical event than a human passage.

However, once the game is up, most terminal patients prefer to pass away at home, at least somewhere away from medical tumult. A hundred years ago, the majority of people died at home. Little could be done for them except see to routine needs, usually by family, friends, and church. People didn't much like to talk about it then; still don't, so dying remains shrouded in mystery. As a total process, it's a transition for family and friends as well as the decedent, occurring in stages, often accompanied by all kinds of issues: legal, financial, cultural, and spiritual.

## Graying Populations

In all advanced economies, graying of the population is obvious not only from statistics, but direct observation. End-of-life healthcare is a social problem everywhere. In advanced economies it's an expensive one because the average person has access to technology for treating extended end-of-life infirmities, thus racking up a high percentage of lifetime health expense. Those that have exhausted curative options receive better palliative care at lower expense in a hospice. The graph below suggests why modern hospice care is growing rapidly.

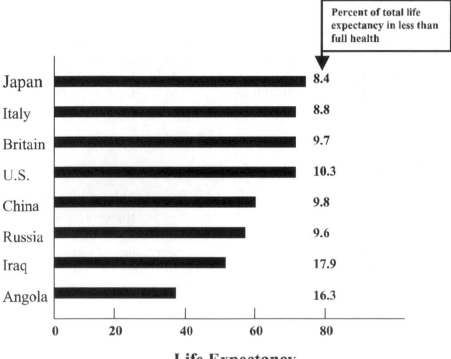

**Life Expectancy**

Data from the World Health Organization. Excerpted from *The Economist*, Dec. 20, 2003, p. 154.

**Figure 1.**

Hospice is a way of shepherding people through this dying process. It is not a place of custodial care. Hospice neither hastens nor prolongs the dying process. Strangely, in so doing it affirms life. The way a modern hospice works is unlike any other organization.

A patient is eligible for hospice care when their attending physician attests that curative treatment is no longer expected to be effective, and that if the condition takes its normal course, they will live no more than another six months. Because the science of such judgments is inexact, some patients live longer than six months. In rare cases, one restores to health and leaves hospice to go on about life. In 2003, the average St. Vincent patient entered hospice care 36 days before death. Some transfer in only a few days or hours before death, usually because of misconceptions about hospice, which the staff regrets. They had too little time to give them the support they deserved.

Medicare and insurance companies favor hospice care too. Nationally, medical expenses in the last year of life average $40,000, with wide variance of course. End-of-life costs consume about 25 percent of all Medicare spending.[3] Medical expenses are lower if a patient's final landing is in hospice. Hospitals concentrate on acute care—very expensive. Nursing homes are less expensive. Least expensive: coaching hospice caregivers at home. About 80 percent of hospice patients are 65 or older. Like "leaning out" operations, it's a better outcome at lower cost.

## The Dying Process

The dying process is unique to each individual. No date or time of death can be exactly predicted. Toward the end, the body prepares to shut down physically, terminating when all physical systems have ceased to function. Most people die in a progression of steps, which is nature's course, and no reason for medical intervention. However, this progression also exhibits much variance. Some persons progress through all stages very quickly; others very slowly; and some skip a phase or two altogether.

An emotional or "spiritual" release process accompanies the physical shutdown, and these two affect each other. The "spirit" of a person prepares to depart its body, its environment, and all attachments. That person may need to resolve unfinished financial business, reconcile close personal relations, or receive permission from family or others to "let go." If important issues are unresolved, he or she will linger—delay shutdown—until they are. For example, a person may hang on for days until someone close to them travels from a distance to say a final good-bye.

The hospice staff coaches family and friends to anticipate these stages before they occur. For example, during physical shutdown, changes in metabolism and an oxygen-deprived brain may make people confused. If they speak they may not make sense. However, talk to them, tell them who's in the room, coming or going. Even if a comatose person appears totally insensate, their sense of hearing is the last to go. Experience at St. Vincent is that both the physical stages and the mental ones (see box below) are general guidelines, not absolute. Patients and families are coached as conditions change.

## Pain and Palliative Care

Palliative care, which includes pain management, is St. Vincent's medical specialty. Terminally ill patients usually experience chronic pain. A drawn countenance indicates pain, but tolerance for it varies greatly, with ones mental and emotional state playing a role. For example, unanticipated pain, as from an accident, is felt more sharply than after a person becomes inured to it. If a victim is in shock, pain will increase as it wears off. The state-of-the-art assessing chronic pain has advanced no further than "Pain is what the patient says it is." St. Vincent uses the standard one to ten scale asking patients to rate pain.

The objective of palliative care is to allow each patient to live to the fullest as long as they can. The staff finds painkiller regimens to make them comfortable, and may use higher doses of morphine. (No point worrying about long-term effects, and contrary to popular belief, addiction to anything properly used to relieve pain is rare.) But patients aren't "zonked"; they prefer them to be as active as possible. Some have projects that they are determined to finish. St. Vincent wants to help patients safely do anything that is important to them.

Alleviation of long-term, intense pain is not in the standard repertoire of physicians practicing curative medicine. For them, pain relief is a temporary fix for a temporary condition. Persistent pain is cause for further examination, and perhaps further treatment. Curative

### Elizabeth Kubler-Ross' Five Stages of Dying

- Denial and isolation (Not me.)
- Anger (Why me?)
- Bargaining (Yes, me... but)
- Depression (Yes, me.)
- Acceptance

Elizabeth Kubler-Ross, probably the best-known student of the dying process, postulated these five emotional stages. Her work in the 1960s stimulated serious study of the dying process, but both her "stage theory" and her studies have been widely criticized since.

physicians are reluctant to prescribe palliatives in high dosages or in combinations, fearing that overdoses or drug dependence might require ancillary treatment—and unwanted reviews by third party providers. But at St. Vincent, pain management, positioning of people and other details add up to making the patient as comfortable as anyone in their plight can be. That's the medical side of palliative care.

However, palliative care also depends on patient environment. Home is almost always the best one if care can be managed there. Patients prefer to see children, pets, and familiar sights, and to have access to activities they like—anything but the sterile décor and procedural bustle of the average medical facility. If they can't stay at home, patients prefer a place that feels like it. St. Vincent's in-patient unit tries to feel like it.

## How St. Vincent Hospice Works

Structurally, St. Vincent's organization resembles other health organizations; multidisciplinary teams and a quality improvement (QI) process are almost expected these days. Technically, it delivers care, just as other organizations deliver products. What sets it apart is that St. Vincent Hospice also cares for relationships.

Neither company nor agency, St. Vincent Hospice is a community united by a common mission. Words like cost, sales, marketing, or even efficiency aren't in the working vocabulary. Instead, within St. Vincent "we" refers to the core of their community, "our network" those they can call on, and "the calling" to the nature of their work.

Figure 2 briefly outlines the operations. In action these are rigorous procedures constantly subject to unexpected events, with which people cope through the give and take of multidisciplinary teamwork.

Typical of the way St. Vincent actually functions is the scheduling of work, done by a committee of three. Each member is experienced in several areas and knows the staff. They meet whenever members' other work responsibilities permit—about once every three weeks. They schedule to an eight-week horizon, each time adding two or three tentative weeks. People occasionally want adjustments, but once a schedule is firm, everyone is expected to meet it. Anyone that can't negotiates a swap with a willing colleague. The schedulers don't hear about this; teamwork gets it done.

*The RF Andon Paging System: St. Vincent is fast answering in-patient call lights. One sampling recorded phenomenal swiftness; response time for five calls averaged 40 seconds—none over a minute.* In hospitals, families must fre-

## Overview of Organization and Operations: St. Vincent Hospice

**In-Patient:**   25-bed capacity; average occupancy varies from 18–23.
Keep two beds open at all times for emergency admissions.
Two nurses stations; two nurses per shift. Average patient/nurse ratio: 5/1

Staffed 24/7/365 with 35 full-time equivalent personnel.

Patients transfer from home when care can no longer be met there—or for short stays when the home caregiver needs a respite.

**Home-Care:**   Average 100 patients in home care; personnel drive to see the patient.
About 80 percent of home care patients are actually at home; the other 20 percent are in extended care facilities, usually nursing homes. Home care is 24/7/365.

Staff: Two teams split coverage of the Indianapolis Metropolitan Area.
A team: five RNs; two social workers; one chaplain.
Average patient/nurse ratio: 10/1 (A ratio beyond 11/1 exceeds capacity.)
Each RN is "on call" one night a week — may not get much sleep.
Two backup RNs are on call weekends; fill in for a regular RN as needed.

An RN, social worker, and chaplain do initial assessment of each patient as the team assigned to that case.
Visits thereafter: RN weekly; social worker and chaplain monthly. But all go as often as needed. Patient needs vary and may change rapidly.

Most home care personnel attend a weekly interdisciplinary team meeting. All cases are discussed biweekly; actions planned.

**Bereavement:**   Most of this is with families, consisting of two kinds of activity:

1.   "Soft touch" interaction.
2.   Regular procedures which can be documented:

   • Bereavement newsletters
   • Scheduled support group sessions
   • Regular monthly phone checks with families for 13 months after the death; extends 24 months after a child's death.
   • Training classes for bereavement volunteers.

About 1,000 families are "somewhere" in this process at all times. Less than 20 percent of them require 80 percent of the attention.

*continued...*

**Figure 2.**

## Overview of Organization and Operations: St. Vincent Hospice

**Pediatric:**       A special unit, but similarly operated. Children require different attention, medically and psychologically. Five to seven children are in hospice at all times. In-patient care is at a nearby children's hospital.

**Physician:**       Dr. Marian McNamara is the medical director, with a back-up in her absence. Some patients transfer from their primary care physician to Dr. McNamara; some don't. Dr. McNamara works with attending physicians, for whom hospice is sometimes a learning experience.

**Social Work:**     Social workers handle non-medical personal issues, everything from insurance and Medicare payments to home maintenance. Families on limited incomes, unfamiliar with "the system" and under stress, consume much of their attention. Elderly caregivers for the dying may not be in good health themselves, and thus need assistance.

**Chaplains:**       The ethos of St. Vincent chaplains is more "be with" than "do for," but sometimes they see to neglected chores like mowing the lawn. Chaplains don't evangelize. Families may adhere to any kind of religion — or none. About 40 percent have no religious affiliation, so chaplains often perform their funeral service. Chaplains are most needed when a family has severe rifts among them to patch over as the patient is dying.

**Volunteers:**      All 250 are unpaid. The volunteer office "hires," trains, coordinates, and monitors all volunteers—and schedules many of them. All new volunteers must finish eight weeks of training, one day a week, before taking any assignment. No retired professionals, like RNs, can continue in that role as a volunteer, but often volunteer to do something else.

Almost 20 percent of St. Vincent's total work hours are by volunteers. The categories of activity break out almost evenly between home care, in-patient care, bereavement, and other. "Other" includes extra touches such as: musical entertainment, pet therapy, massages, and pro bono legal work by volunteer attorneys—and volunteers organize St. Vincent's only annual fundraiser, the Tree of Life observance each December.

To be accredited as a hospice, volunteers must perform at least five percent of all work hours.

**Figure 2.** continued

quently go find a nurse.

Technically, St. Vincent's call paging system is the same as at many other health operations. Opening a secured door or pressing a call button activates both a light over the patient's door and an RF transmitter. Pagers on nurses' belts either ring or vibrate. Looking down, nurses see the room number and its urgency code. The system re-broadcasts the RF page at three-minute intervals until someone deactivates it in the patient's room. Presumably this is a poke-yoke system. Pages can't be ignored.

But they are. Nurses can turn a pager off, and do if it breaks concentration on a task with another patient. Afterward, they may not remember either the page or that the pager is off. And older systems, still in use, only activate lights. Harried nurses may not look at lights for half an hour at a time while who-knows-what is happening to patients. At many hospitals, not answering pages is the most frequent patient and family complaint.

What's different about St. Vincent's call response? The system is simple, units are rarely understaffed, and many people carry pagers. Anyone not locked into a task heads for that room. In addition one of St. Vincent's many volunteers is apt to be on the floor and can watch for things like unanswered lights. No one at St. Vincent can explain how the system technically works. They concentrate on patients and families.[4]

Most hospitals assign only a nurse and an aide to each room, the page goes only to them, and they cover more rooms than at St. Vincent. Overtaxed nurses constantly interrupted by patients' minor whines easily acquire a habit of not minding every page.

Hospitals using a more complex system are generally less effective. If it monitors the activity and location of nurses and aides, they resent it, particularly if they think they are understaffed. There are two lessons here. First, trying to maximize the productivity of people who must respond to emergencies backfires. Second, backup is important, just as each team leader in a lean system should back up every worker. St. Vincent's working culture beats Taylorist efficiency engineering without being efficiency-driven.[5]

## The "Business Model"

"Business model" is not a phrase in vogue at St. Vincent, but works something like this. Patient care operations are paid for by Medicare or third-party providers, and occasionally by patients personally if they have bucks. Charges to third-party providers don't include much over-head because capital and extras come "free" from philanthropy and volunteerism.

Giving is through St. Vincent Foundation, which also serves a par-ent hospital by the same name. Duke Haddad, the executive director, runs a mature philanthropic program, capturing three to five dollars from each one spent in fundraising.

Modest gifts add up, and there are a few large endowments. One, for example, funds landscaping in perpetuity. In 1999 the present building was financed by a capital campaign headed by Rhonda Kittle, whose husband passed away at St. Vincent. Determined that the build-ing layout should come out family-friendly, Mrs. Kittle monitored the architectural planning and construction almost daily.

No wheedling is needed to prompt those that have experienced St. Vincent to give. The attitude of the staff and volunteers *is* St. Vincent. Volunteers add the extras and allow paid staff to concentrate on core care. This combination gives great care at a price Medicare is willing to pay, and good reason for benefactors to part with their money. The working culture is St. Vincent's "business model."

## Getting the Right People on the Bus

Few manufacturing organizations spend the energy to recruit employ-ees that fit in and that have an affinity for the mission. A hospice deals with all kinds of people in the dying process. It isn't for everybody. Both staff and volunteers are as much cultivated as selected. Technical skill should have been demonstrated in a prior job. For example, RNs are hired only after a few years' experience, never right out of school. Young or old, they must be emotionally mature; unflappable; devoid of professional pretension; and ready to give of themselves. Highly prized is sensitive antennae when interacting with the emotional, the confused, and the distressed. Some come to this state after personally tending someone close who died.

But passing these hurdles is not enough. Empathizing with patients starts to become attachment; then they are gone. And no patient tugs the heart more than a dying child. Even some veterans of hospice cannot stomach pediatric care, day after day, year after year, and often at night. That's why the St. Vincent community refers to their work as "the calling" (Figure 3).

The calling sounds religious, but hiring stipulates no religious requirement. Instead it is the ability to do whatever needs doing. For

| **St. Vincent Hospice Mission ...** |
| :--- |
| To provide compassionate holistic care for the dying and those who care for them. |
| "The calling," common to all member institutions of Ascension Health in St. Louis, is prominent in St. Vincent Hospice literature, and printed on every business card: |
| **Service of the Poor:** Generosity of spirit for everyone in need |
| **Reverence:** Respect and compassion for the dignity and diversity of life |
| **Integrity:** Inspiring trust through personal leadership |
| **Wisdom:** Integrating excellence and stewardship |
| **Creativity:** Courageous innovation |
| **Dedication:** Affirming the hope and joy of our ministry. |

**Figure 3.**

instance, a home care nurse must take initiative when necessary, improvising with whatever is at hand, but be patient with caregivers and patients otherwise, and sense when to change an approach. Each day starts at home base; checking overnight logs, mapping five visits for the day, gathering supplies. If everything goes right, work will finish by five. Seldom happens. A patient enters a new phase; takes more time. One not scheduled has an emergency. Another's caregiver has fallen ill; another emergency. Every day God tears up the schedule, but it has to be finished anyway.

Training varies by position, but moves quickly from procedure manuals to working with a preceptor. A watchful preceptor may detect within hours that a new hire has the right stuff—a commitment to the calling—but for others, full commitment comes more gradually. A common path to work up to this is working as a part-timer or temporary (called "PRNs," the medical acronym meaning to take or use when needed).

Volunteer training is thorough. Just as staff, volunteers need to understand the dying process and hospice regulations in order to avoid blundering. Volunteers should be emotionally mature also, and most are, or they would not self-select. Volunteers are evaluated, trained, and assigned a role—then mentored and monitored. Not everyone is cut out for every role, but a hole can be found for every peg. Rebecca Maher, who directs the juggling of all volunteer activity, notes that in ten years only one volunteer could not work out in any role.

Some volunteers "come to work" as regularly as full-time staff, fully dedicated to the calling, and stay active for many years. Others, like the attorneys, or the Spanish translators, have special roles when called on, and critical ones too. Some visit homes to fill in for caregivers who need either to have a break or to run errands.

## Pediatrics

Children are not small adults. St. Vincent's objective is to keep children alive and active as long as possible before the final event. Their medical care and emotional care are different, which is easily seen if children are under school age. Medically, a child with a terminal condition still has the needs and interests of one that is growing normally, while medical status may flip rapidly. For example, one little girl went to school on Thursday and died Friday. By contrast, they may be terribly ill one day and feel ready to do anything the next.

Financial issues are common. A family with young children is apt to live from paycheck to paycheck before disaster strikes. Unless their insurance is unusually generous, it wipes them out. The social worker has to cobble a financial plan together, drawing on resources like The Timmie Foundation (named for a little boy) that specializes in helping the very poor who must choose between keeping the lights on and paying the rent.

Anita Schnaiter, who heads pediatrics, says that cutbacks by third party providers exacerbate financial problems with long-term illness in children. Bills are big; coverage isn't; and the number of cases too limited to grab attention. Each year, only 13–15 children die of natural causes in Indianapolis. Over half enter St. Vincent Hospice.

Emotional issues take the deftest touch. Overwhelmed parents need assurance that they are doing everything they can; things will work out. Siblings need attention if a brother or sister is consuming their parents. Among St. Vincent's extras is a child life specialist, or "play lady," who cheers (and distracts) dying children and their siblings.

All pediatrics staff come to the calling with prior pediatric experience. Only a dozen or so volunteers are up to working with children.

No amount of training instills the right touch for this, but it is insightful. Children know more about life than we give them credit, but not enough to fully comprehend what they are losing. And what do you tell children about dying when anyone they know is dying? The basics when they are ready for them. Being hush-hush brings up a question later, "Why didn't you tell me?"

## Bereavement

Properly conducted, this aspect of hospice care requires broad experience. Nose wiping and handholding are insufficient. The objective is to give therapy to those who need it. People anchored in friendships and activities, experiencing normal grief, need nothing special. Those with pathological grief may deteriorate in both mental and physical health. For example, most of us can recall an older, isolated couple that after one died, the other gave up on life and died soon after. Those are the cases to head off if possible. And children's deaths always call for something extra.

At times the emotions of hospice also "get to" staff members, and they need counseling. All bereavement counselors have taken a difficult grief journey personally; they understand. They cope by having a life outside the calling. Their advice: Live it to the full; do what you like, have a rollicking good time, and leave with no regrets.

Bereavement has become a disciplined practice with ethical standards. The skills needed: assessment, individual counseling (face to face and by telephone), group work, self-awareness, empathy, and patient listening. Both individuals and cultures vary in how they express grief, and it depends on gender, age, spiritual beliefs, and relationship to the deceased. Some crave a group they can open up to; others clam up in stony-faced isolation. Bereavement strives to intervene when needed and how needed.

The crucial skill is listening and observing to deeply understand (sort of a right-brain, behavioral counterpart to TPS leaders standing in Ohno's circle).⁶ Because they are constantly observing, St. Vincent's bereavement staff and volunteers sense things gone wrong, or that a patient or family thinks has gone wrong, anywhere in hospice operations. Every experienced member of the St. Vincent community also does this to some degree. They monitor aspects of quality that data can't describe. Few manufacturing companies would think of developing such a capability.

## The Quality Improvement Meeting

On March 10, 2004, the author attended the monthly meeting of the Quality Improvement Committee, which has ten standing members. All new employees attend a meeting. Anyone important to an issue is invited.

Topics were normal for a quality outfit: Correct unit log processes to assure that when a patient dies, messages to everyone who must be notified are prompt and clear, and the record closes clean. A sub-committee continued to check possible inconsistencies in how home health nurses chart. Med lists on the nursing standards needed updating, etc.

A new after-death family survey form introduced the term "confident" asking ex-caregivers to rate the coaching of home health nurses. They decided that after coaching, nurses should explicitly ask caregivers if they felt "confident" using new procedures.

Survey ratings were high; families grateful for attention score high even if they add nitpick comments. Staff discussed who had time to correlate comments with old charts to dig out specifics they might do better. They bemoaned that surveys only put them on the trail of problems after it was too late to correct them. Then the committee voted to give a token of appreciation to anyone on the staff praised by name on a survey.

No complex methods; no acronyms. Performance isn't "engineered" here. Instead, it's from attention to the precursors of problems in what is happening now, somewhat like Yogi Berra explaining the purpose of batting practice, "Fix it before it happens."

## The Working Culture

St. Vincent excels in soft skills, an area where many manufacturing companies wish they did better. Many people who opt for hospice work have such skills and feel an obligation to practice them, not the case in manufacturing.

St. Vincent works by sustaining relationships with the numerous stakeholders that constitute its community. Manufacturers frequently don't do that well, or do it with only a few external organizations. Within St. Vincent, patients and families come first, of course; then staff, volunteers, donors, other medical institutions, area physicians, other hospices, and on and on. St. Vincent thrives because it "attracts energy" from a broad spectrum of others to the calling, the improve-

## Timeline History of Hospice

**Ancient:** All cultures evolved ways to care for the dying; for example in East Africa, wise elders "saw to" the dying; in ancient China the destitute died in special death houses.

**1500–1800:** Most people died at home. Religious orders cared for those dying alone.

**1800–1900:** Hospitals grew as places of curative treatment. People began to regard dying as a clinical event, but most people still died at home.

**1935:** Hospitals are generally accessible in U.S. towns and cities. Psychosocial studies of dying and bereavement began.

**1967:** St. Christopher's Hospice, the pioneer of modern hospice, opens in London. Care is multidisciplinary. Palliatives are administered at timed intervals, not when "it hurts."

**1974:** Connecticut Hospice becomes the first American hospice to offer home care. Almost all patients who died there had cancer.

**1974–1990:** Hospices expand across North America. Most emphasize home care. In 1982 Medicare adds hospice benefits.

**1990–2004:** The hospice movement expands rapidly. Almost 3000 hospices serve the United States. Patients die of many causes; only half are now cancer patients. But much of the public remains confused about what a modern hospice actually does.

St. Vincent Hospice evolved from a pilot program directed by Margaret Pike from 1978-1981. The official founding was 1982 when the first building opened. The new, larger building opened in 2000.

**Figure 4.**

ment of everyone's experience with the dying process.

St. Vincent is the opposite of a commodity business. They could not garner the same contributions from their stakeholders if they drifted toward a commodity mentality with a profit motive. When the mission is to assuage the final "experience" of each unique patient, plus family and friends, work efficiency is not a conscious consideration. However, waste can be defined: anything we do that interferes with carrying out that mission. Almost subconsciously, the St. Vincent staff pays attention to that.

Consequently, applying examples from St. Vincent to a manu-

### Organizational Vigor Ratings by the A-B-C Framework

This system rates the status of cultural or organizational development on a tough "ivy league" scale. It's not a process examination, like Baldrige, but a working culture development scale. A-B-C is about as precise a scale as can be hoped for. Assumed is that a company has learned techniques for process improvement and implementing innovation.

The bullet points are a few features to look for in each category. F is a failure in any but the cushiest business environment. D (or pre-C) is functional "business as usual," successful through most of the 20th century. C is the first learning stage of a tightly integrated, highly effective operating organization; most lean implementations stop at C class in process improvement. B is a culturally integrated operating business unit; a company can "go for" B Class. A is a capability to strive for, but only after surviving the gales of major change can one be sure of having arrived.

| Class | Process Improvement | Innovation | External Responsibility |
|---|---|---|---|
| A | Process improvement routine; eliminates waste from all-new processes very early. • Very fast learning curves on new products, new technologies, and new processes. | Capable of transforming its industry; can adapt business model to innovate. • Has led a major transition in technology, in markets served, or both. • Has caused customers and others to change behavior. • "Leading edge" | Unified by social mission; serves all stakeholders well; resilient to change/surprise. • Communications with customers and suppliers are open and extensive. • Probably has a relationship-based, novel business model. • Environmental leader. |
| B | Autonomous improvement; embedded in the culture. • Total organization is "lean;" like a "value stream organization." • Process improvement is spontaneous, not directed. • Very low overhead. • Develops or selects customers/suppliers that are also "lean." | Innovate by collaborating; part of everyone's job. • Strong cultural inducements to innovate. • NPD is routine. • Excellent customer insights to stimulate innovation. • Constantly changing. • Good technical information networks are actually used. | "Outside in;" much more customer focused. • Everyone has contact with customers; no customer (or supplier) has difficulty communicating with them. • Very open. Few "secrets." • Everything done makes it easy to work with them. • Environmentally compliant. |
| C | Integrated core operations; directed improvement; still coaching the tools. • "Empowerment" stage. • Metrics are mostly on core operations (plant). • "Blitz" dependent. • Still compare themselves to D class. | Structured new product/ service development; some collaboration. • Has a "gated" NPD process. • Cross-functional teams used for development. • Understanding of customer may be from a distance. • NPD still "disruptive." | Serves customers well; great quality, efficiency, and delivery. • Do what they promise, but few extras impress customers or other stakeholders. • Customer-oriented, but not customer-inviting. |
| D or Pre-C | Process improvement is fragmented; any integration is engineered by a system. | Minimal integration of NPD; probably "over the wall." No systemic promotion of innovation. | Concentrate on the customer; no special regard for other stakeholders. Regard many external relations as "win-lose." |
| F | Random and reactionary; poorly organized operations. | Reactionary; sporadic attention to it is ineffective. | Inward-centered; customer service is erratic. |

facturing company's operations requires translation—and rumination. It relates to "Respect of People," that other "pillar" of the Toyota Way, which Toyota breaks down further: 1) Respect others; make every effort to understand each other; take responsibility; and do our best to build mutual trust. And 2) Teamwork: Stimulate personal and professional growth; share opportunities for develop-

### St. Vincent Hospice A-B-C Rating:

| Class | Process Improvement | Innovation | External Responsibility |
|-------|--------------------|-----------|-------------------------|
| **A** | | | X |
| **B** | X | X | |
| **C** | | | |

**Notes**: St. Vincent Hospice is not a commercial company, nor does it behave as one.

**Process Improvement**: Organizationally, St. Vincent operations are very well integrated. Core personnel know each other; informal communication supplements formal systems; and they meet emergency demands by "calling in their reserves." Training is thorough; standards well developed and adhered to. Their ethos: do whatever it takes to see each patient out in comfort and with dignity. Procedural improvement happens because people see that it's necessary for their mission, not because of a rigorous improvement methodology. Much of the time their ethos leads them to a good process without the assistance of formal improvement tools. Rating: Low B.

**Innovation**: Improvisation occurs daily. In home health nursing, this may take the form of rigging devices to help the patient, using whatever is at hand, but much of it is behavioral. Personnel are keen sensing and intervening appropriately when patients and their families need it. They keep up with the latest methods in both palliative and behavioral care and test them, and St. Vincent is beginning to be an innovator that other hospices come to study. Low B here.

**External Responsibility**: One would be hard pressed to find an organization more symbiotic with the needs of a metropolitan community than St. Vincent Hospice. Patients enter St. Vincent because they hear about it from people that have experienced St. Vincent: the corps of volunteers, the army of families of ex-patients, and personnel of other medical institutions that transfer patients to them. By example, not advertising, they are dispelling the public's misconceptions about hospice care. In this they are outstanding. In other areas such as environmental disposal, they are compliant, but not a leader. An A here.

ment; and maximize individual and team performance. That describes St. Vincent Hospice.

## Leadership

No one can lead an organization like this without walking the path of the calling with everyone else. Ferne Squiers is St. Vincent's new director. Ask others what she does, and the likely response is, "role model." Prior directors were role models.

Ask Ferne Squiers what she does, and first priority is "quality of all the care we provide." Yes, she battles budgets and financial stability, freeing others to carry out the mission. She deals with all regulatory issues and processes. And she represents St. Vincent Hospice to all the rest of the world. But what does it take to do this job? "I cannot separate my hospice from my personal life," is her reply. Another lesson to think about.

*Robert W. Hall is editor-in-chief of* Target *and a founding member of AME.*

### Footnotes

1. The Toyota Way is the company's articulation of its core values as a company, and not the same as the twin-pillared building Toyota often uses when explaining the basis of the Toyota Production System.
2. A typical article addressing this issue is "G.M. Says Costs for Retiree Care Top $60 Billion," *New York Times,* March 12, 2004.
3. According to Donald Hoover, a statistician at Rutgers University, based on surveys and national healthcare statistics.
4. Information about paging systems is from Mike Zeiss, Circuit Master, Indianapolis, who installs and maintains these systems for many healthcare facilities. The pagers are not regular telephone pagers, but customized for this application using the POGSAG special protocol. The RF broadcast has a range of two miles, so nurses will receive a page even if they are in the parking lot. These systems began to be installed about 20 years ago, and have gradually added features. However, the complex ones are more expensive, more troublesome to program and maintain, and seldom stay in service more than a year.
5. Nurses' resentment of Taylorist management in hospitals is a long-standing issue, studied many times. Nurses are apt to refer to Taylorism as constraining or restrictive of quality care. A typical survey is Chapter 5 of Nurse Abuse, by Laura Gasparis and Joan Swirsky, Power Publications, Staten Island, NY, 1993.
6. See "Ohno's Method," Robert W. Hall, *Target,* Q1, 2002, pp. 6-15.

## Questions

Does your organization embody the principle of respect for people?

Do you use multi-disciplinary teams? Do those teams handle scheduling?

How quickly does your staff respond to in-patient call lights?

Do you have processes for cultivating skills in your staff?

Do your staffers constantly observe what is happening, and are they able to sense when something is wrong?

Do you survey customers (patients or families) after the completion of service (care)?

Do you have a system for rating your organization in areas such as process improvement and innovation?

# Index

Accounts payable
  lean process for, 36–37
  unnecessary paperwork in, 48–49
Admin cell
  for inquiries, 55–56
  issues with, 56–57
  success of, 57–58
Administrative environment
  lean success in, 51–62
  production v., 51–52
  workforce in, vii
Adulthood. See Murray/Adulthood
AME. See Association for Manufacturing
  Excellence
Andon lights, for patient safety, 100
Antioch Company
  about, 30, 50n1
  accounts payable project at, 36–37
  capital expense request process at, 37
  lean process and, 34–39
  office waste uncovered at, 41–50
  process mapping at, 35
  6S program at, 49, 50n2
  sharing experiences at, 37–38
  visualizing, implementing improvements
    at, 35–36
Association for Manufacturing Excellence
  (AME)
  in service industry, viii
  Target of, xi
Audit process, of 5S procedure, 81–82
Awareness
  for lean office, 63–65
  from lean office events, 44–45, 69

Baldridge Award, resources for, 104
Behavior
  from metrics, 66
  process excellence in, 109
Bereavement, at St. Vincent Hospice, 121
Bill of material (BOM), metrics for, 65
BOM. See Bill of material
Boston Scientific. See Guidant
Brainstorming
  "postponed perfection" from, 56
  "trystorming" v., 55
Bridges to Excellence
  overview of, 106
  resources for, 104
"Business model," at St. Vincent Hospice,
  117–18

Call response
  at hospitals, 117, 126n4
  at St. Vincent Hospice, 114–17
"The Calling," St. Vincent Hospice, 109–27
Cancer Treatment Centers of America, lean
  thinking at, 101
Capital expense request process, lean process
  for, 37
CBD teams. See Customer Business

Development teams
Centralized office workflow system, at
  Waukesha Bearings, 59–60
CI. See Continuous improvement
Coaching, at HUI, 6
Co-location, in lean process, 20–22
Communication, from lean office events, 45,
  67–69
Consumer-Purchaser Disclosure Project
  for healthcare performance information,
    103–4
  resources for, 104
Continuous improvement (CI)
  ICR for, 31
  starting small, 19
  at Steelcase, 18–19
  of TPS, 109
Control systems, in lean thinking, ix
Corporate culture, ICR and, 33
Critical Success Factors (CSFs), for hospital
  error reduction, 101–2
Cross-functional changes, in lean office initiatives, 12
CSFs. See Critical Success Factors
CT scans, lean processes for, 94–95
Cultural change
  at Elgin Sweeper Company, 75, 77
  in healthcare, 89–108
  in lean process, 21, 23
Customer Business Development teams (CBD
  teams)
  hiring with, 8
  at HUI, 7–8
  improvement in, 8–9
Customer satisfaction
  classification of, viii–ix
  group for, 23
Customer service
  PDM improvement of, 19–20
  reorganization for, 16–18
Customer-focused lean, at Steelcase, 11–25
Customers
  learning from, 22–23
  patients treated as, 90–93

Decision making, for long-term improvement,
  3
Decision panel, in lean process, 13–14
Delivery time, metrics for, 65
Dying process
  in history, 110
  in hospice care, 111–12
  overview of, 112–13
  stages of, 113

EI. See Employee involvement
Electronic documentation, in PDM, 20
Elgin Sweeper Company
  about, 76
  5S events at, 77–79
  audit process at, 81–82

lean enterprise system at, 76–77
lean in office environment at, 81, 83
lean operations at, 75–85
lessons learned at, 81–84
training at, 79–80
E-mails, lean office event and unnecessary, 48–49
Employee involvement (EI), in lean operations, 75
Experience, learning from, 22–23

Facilitators, for lean office events, 68–70
Follow-up meetings, for lean process, 71

Gemba walks, at Steelcase, 12
Goals
    for 5S event, 79
    for lean office event, 69
    in lean thinking, 3
Graphics department, lean process and, 21–23, 70
Graying populations, 111
Guidant, lean thinking at, viii

Health Policy Corporation of Iowa (HPCI)
    healthcare conference by, 93
    Hot Team and, 93–94
    lean enterprise conference by, 93
Healthcare
    CSFs for hospital error reduction, 101–2
    IHI and, 91
    improving service in, 92
    insurance providers and, 96–98
    in Iowa, 93–94
    lean thinking reduces errors in, 101
    patient safety in, 100–101
    peg buys to quality in, 106–7
    reducing errors and waste in, 102–3
    TPS for, 92, 98
    transformation of, 89–108
    transparency in, 103–6
    zero defects through TPS in, 98–100
HealthGrades, resources for, 104
Hiring
    at HUI, 8
    at St. Vincent Hospice, 118–19
Hospice care
    dying process at, 112–13
    growth of, 110–12
    overview of, 109–10
    pain and palliative care at, 113–14
    timeline history of, 123
    working of, 114–17
Hospital
    call response at, 117
    CSFs for error reduction at, 101–2
    hospice v., 110
    taylorism in, 126n5
Hot Team
    additional collaboration with, 95–96

for Iowa hospital kaizen events, 93–94
    projects of, 95–96
HPCI. *See* Health Policy Corporation of Iowa
HUI
    about, 4
    additional transitions at, 8–9
    improvement model at, 4–6
    leadership and coaching at, 6
    lean process and, 3–10
    lessons learned at, 10
    office team results at, 9
    organizational structure at, 6–8
    true change at, 9
    values at, 4–5

ICR. *See* Integrated Cost Reduction
Idea Qualification Level (IQL), ICR and, 32
IHA. *See* Iowa Hospital Association
IHI. *See* Institute for Healthcare Improvement
Institute for Healthcare Improvement (IHI)
    100k Lives Campaign of, 91
    resources for, 105
Insurance provider
    building trust of, 96–98
    hospice care and, 112
Integrated Cost Reduction (ICR)
    for CI, 31
    corporate culture and, 33
    IQL and, 32
    overview of, 30–31
    at Rockwell Automation, 29–30
    targets for, 31–32
Interruptions, in PDM, 19–20
Iowa Business Council
    Hot Team and, 93–94
    lean enterprise conference by, 93
Iowa Chamber of Commerce, Hot Team and, 93–94
Iowa Coalition for Innovation and Growth
    healthcare improvements and, 96
    Hot Team and, 93–94
Iowa Department of Public Health, healthcare conference by, 93
Iowa, healthcare in, 93–94
Iowa Hospital Association (IHA), healthcare conference by, 93
Iowa Medical Association, healthcare conference by, 93
Iowa Nurses Association, healthcare conference by, 93
IQL. *See* Idea Qualification Level

JIT. *See* Just-In-Time
Just-In-Time (JIT), dispatch system, 99

Kaizen
    at Antioch Company, 34
    examples of, ix
    in healthcare, 95–96

LAC. *See* Lean action committee
Leadership
    at HUI, 6
    at St. Vincent Hospice, 126
Lean action committee (LAC), at Steelcase, 12
Lean concepts
    at Cancer Treatment Centers of America,
        101
    in HUI improvement model, 4–5
    in office, 64–65
    organization-wide, 98
Lean enterprise system (LES)
    at Elgin Sweeper Company, 76–77
    results of, 84
Lean initiatives
    before and after, 61
    experiences from, 37–38
    for healthcare, 92
    structure for, 12–15
    of ThedaCare, 90
Lean movement
    for inquiry process, 55–56
    at Waukesha Bearings, 52–54
Lean office
    analyze metrics for, 65
    awareness for, 63–65
    getting started with, 68–70
    lessons learned, 72
    mapping your way to change, 63–73
    questions for, 64
    sustaining, 71–72
    updating metrics, 66–68
Lean Office Department
    at Antioch Company, 41–43
    development of, 49
Lean office event
    at Antioch Company, 41–50
    benefits of, 42
    concept of, 42–43
    getting started with, 68–70
    lack of awareness and, 44–45
    lack of communication and, 45
    lack of training and, 48
    metrics for, 65
    poor process flow and, 46–47, 69
    preparation for, 34–35
    priceless knowledge, team solutions,
        41–50
    process owner and, 47
    rules for, 43–44, 68–69
    steps of, 67
    unnecessary paperwork and, 48–49
    wastes uncovered by, 44–45, 52–54
Lean operations, benefits of, 75
Lean project phases, at Steelcase, 13–14
Lean Steering Committee, at Elgin Sweeper
        Company, 76
Lean success, in administrative environment,
        51–62
Lean training

    at Elgin Sweeper Company, 79–80
    at HUI, 8
    need for, 38
    at Steelcase, 18–19
Leapfrog Group
    about, 97
    insurance providers and, 97
    resources for, 105
LES. *See* Lean enterprise system
Life expectancy, 110–11
Logs, lean office event and unnecessary, 48–49

Management structure, as obstacle, 6–7
Manufacturing industry
    lean thinking in, vii
    workforce in, vii
Manufacturing process maps, description of,
        16
Marketing, for long-term improvement, 3
Maytag, VSM program at, 93
Metrics
    analyzing, 65
    at HUI, 9
    for long-term improvement, 3
    at Steelcase, 21–22
    of ThedaCare, 92
    updating, 66–68
    at Waukesha Bearings, 56
Muda, mapping of, 16–17
Murray/Adulthood
    concepts of, 5–6
    in HUI improvement model, 4–6
    overview of, 5

National Business Coalition on Health
        (NBCH), overview of, 106
National Patient Safety Foundation, resources
        for, 105
National Quality Forum (NQF), resources for,
        105
NBCH. *See* National Business Coalition on
        Health
Non-value-added steps (NVA)
    elimination of, 63, 69, 94
    in PDM, 19–20
    in process mapping, 35
    removal of, 17
    at Wellmark Blue Cross Blue Shield, 97–98
NQF. *See* National Quality Forum
NVA. *See* Non-value-added steps

Office environment, lean in, 81, 83
Office lean consulting team (OLCT), at
        Steelcase, 12
Office lean teamwork
    of accounts payable, 36–37
    of capital expense request process, 37
    at HUI, 3–4
    lessons learned about, 22
    production v., 24

suggestions for, 24–25
work in progress of, 9
Office processes
kaizen of, ix
maps of, 16
NVA elimination in, 63
OLCT. *See* Office lean consulting team
100k Lives Campaign
of IHI, 91
ThedaCare and, 92
One-piece flow
at VMMC, 99–100
at Waukesha Bearings, 59–60
Opportunity Log, in 5S program, 79
Order creation, lean process for, 61
Order entry system, kaizen of, ix
Organizational strategy, for long-term
improvement, 3
Organizational structure
at HUI, 6–8
for long-term improvement, 3
as obstacle, 6–7
Organizational vigor ratings, at St. Vincent
Hospice, 124
Overhead, reductions in, 9

Pain care, in hospices, 113–14
Palliative care, in hospices, 113–14
Patience, for lean process, 23–24
Patient
call response for, 114–17
safety of, 100–101
treating as customer, 90–93
Patient Safety Alert System (PSAS), at
VMMC, 100
PDCA. *See* Plan, Do, Check, Act
PDM. *See* Product Data Management
Pediatrics, at St. Vincent Hospice, 120–21
Photocopies, lean office event and unneces-
sary, 48–49, 69
Plan, Do, Check, Act (PDCA), in lean process,
15, 21
"Postponed perfection," from brainstorming,
56
Process flow, lean office events and poor,
46–47, 69
Process maps
about, 69
of accounts payable, 36–37
at Antioch Company, 35
improvements from, 35–36
for lean office event, 42–43
manufacturing v. office, 16
use of, 16–17
Process owner, lean office event and, 47
Product Data Management (PDM), at
Steelcase, 19–20
Product development
ICR for, 31
training for, 48

Production floor
administrative environment v., 51–52
lean process beyond, 29–39
Production lean teamwork, office v., 24
Project managers, in lean process, 14
PSAS. *See* Patient Safety Alert System
Pull system, based on customer need, 95

Quality improvement meeting, at St. Vincent
Hospice, 122

Rapid Process Improvement Workshop
(RPIW), at VMMC, 99
"Respect for People," of TPS, 109, 125–26
Retirement plans, competitiveness and, 110,
126n2
Rework
with PDM, 19–20
with poor process flow, 46–47, 69
Risk-taking, encouragement of, 3
Rockwell Automation
about, 30
improvement target selection, 31–32
leadtime, cost, and inventory reduction
targets, 29–34
lessons learned at, 33–34
mind set for change, 33
RPIW. *See* Rapid Process Improvement
Workshop
Rules, for lean office event, 43–44, 68–69

5S program
blitz process in, 78
at Cancer Treatment Centers of America,
101
at Elgin Sweeper Company, 75–77
logistics checklist for, 78
operation of, 77–79
overview of, 80
training for, 79–80
at VMMC, 99–100
6S program
at Antioch Company, 49, 50n2
at Waukesha Bearings, 57
Senior leadership, support of, 11–12
Service industry
customer in, viii
examples of, viii
lean thinking in, viii
workforce in, vii
SFT. *See* Solutions Fulfillment Team
Shop floor teaming
at HUI, 3–4
knowledge from, 6–7
Shop floor, work flow on, vii
Simpler Conversion, for lean consulting, 52
Solutions Fulfillment Team (SFT)
starting small, 18–19
at Steelcase, 16–17
St. Vincent Hospice

bereavement at, 121
"business model" at, 117–18
growth of hospice care, 110–12
leadership at, 126
lean thinking in, viii
mission of, 119
operations of, 114–17
organizational vigor ratings at, 124
pediatrics at, 120–21
quality improvement meeting at, 122
right people on board at, 118–20
"The Calling," 109–27
working culture at, 122–26
Standard work instructions (SWIs), at Cancer
     Treatment Centers of America, 101
State maps, types of, 54
Steelcase
     gaining traction, 24–25
     implementing customer-focused lean,
          11–25
     learning from experience, customers,
          22–23
     lessons learned, 23–24
     PDM at, 19–20
     reorganization for better customer service,
          16–18
     senior leadership support, 11–12
     start small, 18–19
     starting the evolution, 20–22
     structure for lean initiatives at, 12–15
     value stream mapping and visual control
          at, 15–17, 23
Strategic position, in HUI improvement
     model, 4–5
SWIs. See Standard work instructions

Target
     of AME, xi
     lean thinking in, viii
Taylorism, in hospitals, 126n5
ThedaCare
     100k Lives Campaign and, 92
     lean efforts of, 90–93
     savings by, 92
Toyota Production System (TPS)
     for healthcare, 92, 98
     overview of, 126n1
     questions of, 15
     "Respect for People" of, 109, 125–26
     takeoff from, vii
TPS. See Toyota Production System
Training, lean office event and lack of, 48
Triage abandonment rates, in healthcare, 91
"Trystorming," in lean movement, 55–56

UIHC. See University of Iowa Hospitals and
     Clinics
University of Iowa Hospitals and Clinics
     (UIHC), lean processes at, 94–95

VA. See Value-added activities
Value engineering team (VE team), IQL with,
     32
Value stream manager, in lean process, 13
Value stream mapping (VSM)
     at Cancer Treatment Centers of America,
          101
     lessons learned about, 22–23
     by Maytag, 93
     "outsiders" input in, 54
     in RPIW, 99
     at Steelcase, 15–17, 23
     three-day event for, 52–54
     visual process control with, 16
     at Waukesha Bearings, 52
Value-added activities (VA), in process map-
     ping, 35
Values, at HUI, 4–5
VE team. See Value engineering team
Virginia Mason Medical Center (VMMC)
     5S program at, 99–100
     patient safety at, 100–101
     RPIWs at, 99
     seeking zero defects at, 98–100
Visual control
     at Steelcase, 15–17
     with VSM, 16
VMMC. See Virginia Mason Medical Center
VSM. See Value stream mapping

Waste
     attack on, 63–64
     in hospice care, 124
     reduction in healthcare, 102–3
     UIHC removal of, 94–95
     uncovered with lean office events, 44–45,
          52–54
Waukesha Bearings Ltd.
     before and after at, 61
     concluding remarks on, 61–62
     concurrent one-piece flow, 59–60
     habit keeping, 60–61
     lean process at, 51
     not quite a showcase, 55–56
     one step back, 56–57
     slow out of blocks, 52–53
     three-day VSM event, 52–54
     two steps forward, 57–59
Wellmark Blue Cross Blue Shield
     doing business with, 96–98
     eliminating NVA activities at, 97–98
Whiteboard, as lean process resource, 56–57
Work flow
     control system for, 58–59
     redesign, 101
     on shop floor, vii
Workforce, division of, vii
Working culture, at St. Vincent Hospice,
     122–26
Workload, sharing, 59–60